NOLA FACE

SERIES EDITOR

Nicole Walker

SERIES ADVISORY BOARD

Steve Fellner
Kiese Laymon
Lia Purpura
Paisley Rekdal
Wendy S. Walters
Elissa Washuta

NOLA FACE

》》》》》》》《《《《《《《《

A LATINA'S
LIFE IN THE
BIG EASY

》》》》》》》《《《《《《《《

BROOKE
CHAMPAGNE

THE UNIVERSITY OF
GEORGIA PRESS
ATHENS

Published by the University of Georgia Press
Athens, Georgia 30602
www.ugapress.org
© 2024 by Brooke Champagne
All rights reserved
Designed by Kaelin Chappell Broaddus
Set in 10.75/13.5 Fournier MT Std Regular by Kaelin Chappell Broaddus
Printed and bound by Sheridan Books, Inc.
The paper in this book meets the guidelines for permanence
and durability of the Committee on Production Guidelines
for Book Longevity of the Council on Library Resources.

Most University of Georgia Press titles are
available from popular e-book vendors.

Printed in the United States of America
24 25 26 27 28 P 5 4 3 2 1

Library of Congress Cataloging-in-Publication Data

Names: Champagne, Brooke, 1980– author.
Title: Nola face : a Latina's life in the big easy / Brooke Champagne.
Other titles: Latina's life in the big easy
Description: Athens : The University of Georgia Press, [2024] |
Series: Crux : the Georgia series in literary nonfiction
Identifiers: LCCN 2023039661 | ISBN 9780820366531 (paperback) |
ISBN 9780820366548 (epub) | ISBN 9780820366555 (pdf)
Subjects: LCSH: Champagne, Brooke, 1980– | Hispanic American women—
Louisiana—New Orleans—Biography. | Racially mixed women—Louisiana—
New Orleans—Biography. | Ecuadorian Americans—Louisiana—New Orleans—
Biography. | New Orleans (La.)—Social life and customs—20th century. |
New Orleans (La.)—Biography.
Classification: LCC F379.N553 C423 2024 | DDC 976.3/35092 [B]—dc23/eng/20230905
LC record available at https://lccn.loc.gov/2023039661

For Brock and Mina and Manny

Verde que te quiero verde.
Bajo la luna gitana,
las cosas la están mirando,
y ella no puede mirarlas.

—from "Romance Sonámbulo,"
Federico García Lorca

There are a lot of places I like,
but I like New Orleans better. . . .
The city is one very long poem.

—from *Chronicles: Volume One*, Bob Dylan

You will never write a book.

—from Turd, the man who read my tarot cards
outside Molly's at the Market

CONTENTS

ACKNOWLEDGMENTS

My big ol' family, who both made me and are forced to put up with this person they made, deserves first mention. I love you endlessly and thank you for letting me write about us. Or for skipping the stuff you'd rather not remember.

New Orleans, I'd say *get it together* but we both know that's never happening. As ever, I adore you anyway.

Thank you to series editor Nicole Walker for selecting *Nola Face* and championing it fiercely. Thanks to Beth Snead and everyone at Crux and UGA Press for a downright joyful first-book experience.

I'm also grateful to the journal editors who published excerpts from the book. You not only promoted my essays but improved them in large and small ways I couldn't have imagined. Thanks for your keen eyes and warm hearts.

My friends provide boundless inspiration and love. Holly Hudson and Rob Dixon and Ginger Baker and Carl Peterson, thank you for somehow knowing when to ask how the writing's going versus when to offer a hug or a shot. Thank you for being my cherished chosen family.

To my girls across time and distance, who read pages and offered support and cried and laughed with me: Ashley Arceneaux, Lisa Tallin, Karen Gardiner, Natalie Loper, Jessica Kidd, Courtney George, Amy Monticello, Danielle O'Sullivan, Marsha McSpadden, Nalia King, Kris Hoang, and Gloria Mitchell. Near, or far, or gone, you're always with me.

To the teachers who believed in my work and found worthiness when I couldn't: Margie St. Pierre, David Middleton, Rodger Kamenetz, and Andrei Codrescu.

My esteemed students and colleagues in the English Department at the University of Alabama influence my thinking, these pages, and my life. RMFT.

To my outrageously talented and generous writing group, Ruth Gila Berger, Sydney Tammarine, and Michelle Valenti. Thank you, my queens, for reigning in the land of Supreme Cunts.

My sisters, I could've been a better eldest to the four of you, but how much fun would that have been? Thanks for leading the way in motherhood, for knowing me the way no one else can, and for loving me despite all that. Brittany, we miss you more than words can say.

Mom, you gave me life, you gave me milk, and you gave me the patience, strength, and good humor required for survival. I cannot apologize enough for ages twelve to seventeen, and I hope to spend the rest of my years making it up to you. Momma, you are beloved on this earth.

Dad, if you're reading this, you've reached way too far into the book. Though by now I hope you know that you're the perfect father for me. Thanks for your wit, your crazy wisdom, and your stories, delivered in a way only you can. I expect many more in years to come.

Mi Mami Lala, santificada sea tu nombre. Cada dia te extraño.

Mina and Manny, mis pollitos, you are my reason for everything. I love you beyond measure, plus I also like you. Thank you to the cosmic forces who brought us these two most precious, tremendous gifts. I will kiss your beauty marks for the rest of my days, or until my lips fall off.

To Brock, my first and best reader: this book, and everything I hold dear about this life, starts and ends with you. Thank you for your love, your steadfastness, your words, and thank you for choosing me every day. My buggy boy, I choose you, too.

The following essays (or earlier versions of them) appear in journals, as follows:

"Cielito Lindo" in *Hunger Mountain Review*
"Three Sacraments" in *New Ohio Review*
"Pipón" in *Florida Review*
"What I Know about the Chicken Lady" in *Los Angeles Review*
"McCleaning with the Dustbuster" in *Full Grown People*
"Lying in Translation" in *Bending Genre*
"Push" in *Cherry Tree*
"Kingdom of Babes" in *Hoxie Gorge Review*
"The Stump of *The Giving Tree*" in *Allium: A Journal of Prose & Poetry*
"Don't You Forget about Me" in *Miracle Monocle*
"Exercises" in *Normal School*
"Nice Lady" in *Under the Sun*
"Bugginess" in *Chattahoochee Review*
"An Essay Entitled 'Mrs.'" in *Waxwing*
"How Not to Hate Your Writing" in *Emrys Journal*
"Bobbitt" in *Barrelhouse*
"The Case for 'Cunt'" in *Full Grown People*
"Nola Face" in *Tahoma Literary Review*

A NOTE FROM THE AUTHOR

This is a work of nonfiction. Memory's many vagaries, discussed frequently throughout the book, continue to challenge and delight my writing process. That said, I have taken great care to remain faithful to the past as I remember it and render as honestly as memory allows the people and events that appear in these pages. In order to protect their privacy, I have changed certain names and identifying characteristics.

≫⟩ ≫⟩ ≫⟩ ≫⟩ ≫⟩ ⟨≪ ⟨≪ ⟨≪ ⟨≪ ⟨≪

PART I

TWO TRUTHS AND A LIE

AN INTRODUCTION

≫⟩ ≫⟩ ≫⟩ ≫⟩ ≫⟩ ⟨≪ ⟨≪ ⟨≪ ⟨≪ ⟨≪

I began teaching college at LSU in Baton Rouge, an hour northwest of my hometown, when I was still college-aged myself. I'd been raised with the eighties and nineties pop culture certainty that those who couldn't do, taught. But no John Hughes film, with its perverted gym teachers or slit-eyed administrators, could shame me. Instead, when given the opportunity to teach, I thought, "my perfect job." Because it was true, I *couldn't* do anything else. Or at least, I didn't want to try. I'd applied to graduate writing programs straight out of college since telling and listening to stories was my singular affinity. My New Orleans upbringing inhered a loafing, patrilineal tradition that insisted ambition was for capitalist shits; if you wanted, my French-Sicilian father could tell you all about it over a cocktail or eight. Plus, this job for the talentless offered health insurance, another capitalist necessity I couldn't have otherwise afforded, so who was the sucker? Anyway, how hard could it be?

Oh, I learned. In those first few teaching years, many times while driving to campus, I secularly prayed for a minor car accident. I didn't want to maim anyone, or myself, but needed a day-pass from teaching. It's difficult facing your failures before a group of people who don't respect you and, worse, don't have a reason to. Once, a student balked during a lesson in which I used my dogs as a writing metaphor. "Try to strike a delicate balance in your essayist persona," I'd said. "Who are you on the page? What's your writerly voice?" She asked me to explain further, but I couldn't. First of all, I didn't fully understand the concepts of persona or voice yet, nor could I get across my sense as either writer or teacher that the Platonic ideal of the golden retriever is a paradox, because if you're beloved by every student, are you really teaching them anything? Similarly, if your writing is beloved by all, are you really saying anything? Or are you just a blonde, vanilla, fluffy version of a writer whose personality is "nice"? I unsuccessfully tried connecting these dots in the classroom and received a roomful of Rottweiler stares in response.

Back then, I aspired in my own writing for a delicate balance between my Australian shepherd, King (diffident, elusive, neurotic), and Nola, a rescue mutt (playful, curious, charmingly bullish). It gives me douche chills remembering this now, but I even showed them an essay draft about my *loca* Ecuadorian grandmother, Lala, as an example of writing that worked (as opposed to theirs, which clearly didn't). Their written grandmothers, and the students' perspectives of them, came off bland. "Amazing." "Loving." "Selfless." Ugh. Where was the regret, the hurt, the skin, the teeth? How to teach "be more interesting"?

A blonde beauty queen, who I'd become allergic to on first sight, spoke up. "Hey Miss, are you sure you own dogs and not cats?"

"Yes, I've shown you their pictures—on the ironically titled Power-Point 'Avoiding Wordiness at All Costs.' Why would you think I own cats?"

"Because cats suck."

She didn't have to be such a little cunt about it, but I had to agree with her. Both cats and I sucked. I was a terrible teacher. Rather than seeing the potential in their work, how an essay or story might take shape, I mostly reminded students how their writing missed the mark. Besides, I was beginning to wonder, who were we kidding— could writing even be taught? Especially when I myself was still, you know, not great at it. Any loathing of their work was just thinly veiled self-loathing of mine. I regularly embarrassed myself in those early years, only half-understanding the subject of my supposed expertise. Though it's true, I never whiffed it as badly as my fiction-writer friend Ashley when she got stuck teaching poetry, a genre with which she had zero familiarity. She walked in on the first day of Critical Approaches to Poetry and somewhere in her bewildered opening, impressed by her awareness of "canon," said, "So, Sappho, we'll start next class period with him, he's an extremely *canonical* poet." One of her students interjected to say Sappho was one of the first great lyric *female* poets, from the island of Lesbos, and yes, *she* was canonical. What else could any of us do? Sometimes, we were morons. Often, we sucked. Still, we taught anyway.

In the years since, I've found some rapport with teaching, once I realized it was a performative game. I've learned to play the role of expert-cum-doofus. My teaching persona is metadeliberative, vacillates between conviction and doubt, shares deeply personal stories full of self-admitted folly (like the one where the blonde implied I sucked and that, despite her bitchiness, I agreed with her—students eat these stories up). In this voice, any fuckup feels preordained, which makes me more trustworthy to students. This, folks, is called ethos.

Like most people, I suppose, I appreciate relationships, both in and out of the classroom, that deepen and complicate over time, but the first day of teaching in any semester, when I know jack-shit about my students, is still my favorite. I could be anyone, and so could they: we still hide behind our infinite masks. Plus, it's sanctioned icebreaker time. An early beloved game was Two Truths and a Lie. For those uninitiated, the rules: students must write, then read aloud, three statements about themselves, and their peers must guess which of the statements is a lie.

My most memorable experience playing Two Truths and a Lie was my very first. A curly haired, blue-eyed Latina student volunteered to start us off. Here was her list:

1. The first and last time I went skydiving,
   my parachute almost didn't open.
2. I'm Mexican.
3. I've broken a dozen bones in my body.

Her lie was, of course, "I'm Mexican." Yes, she was brown skinned, clearly Latina, but her parents were Colombian. I fell in love with this lie, because in composing it, she was betting her mostly white peers would presume any statement made about her ethnicity was genuine;

or, they'd be afraid to question it; or, they'd see her brown skin and go, sure, makes sense, Mexican. She predicated her lie on her assumptions about audience, which became the common rationale for hundreds of students' lies across the years. (The lie from an ostentatiously queer kid: "I'm 100 percent straight." One from an older, nontraditional German student: "This class is, how do you say it, my first rodeo?"). Later in that very first class, my Latina student admitted her eyes were also lies—she wore cornflower-blue-colored contacts. Discovering truths behind facades is one of teaching's, and life's, great surprises and joys.

Come to think of it, it's been awhile since I played Two Truths and a Lie in the classroom. Asking students to divulge parts of their identity or story when they might not be ready is more of a fifth classroom-date rhetorical move these days, so we ease into them more slowly; I don't want to disturb any sensitivities at first sight. Now, so that I can memorize everyone's names on day one, I'll usually play the Name Game.[1] It's my go-to, because if I can immediately call students by their names, they will believe, even if it's not yet true, that I know and deeply care about them. But I miss how Two Truths and a Lie delves into both how we see ourselves and how we expect others to see us, which makes playing it with you, reader (in a slightly more elaborate and essayistic version), a good primer for this book of personal essays.

(1) While I was working on my thesis in graduate school—a memoir about my abuela, Lala, who you'll soon come to know—a poet friend said to me, "You'd better hurry up and finish your book . . ." Let me interrupt the latter part of her sentence so I can express how I initially hoped she'd complete it. I wanted her to say, "because the world needs it," or more realistically, "because I want to read it," or even,

---

1 The rules: the student seated at the desk closest to me introduces themself, and then the next person in the row introduces themself and the person who came before, and on and on until the person in the back corner, sitting furthest away from me, is asked to introduce themself and everyone else, and unless they have excellent memories, wishes they'd skipped that day. I always play last and ask students to randomly raise their hands so that I can say their names out of order (thus making the task more difficult). In all these years, I've never forgotten a name.

"because you're good." But here's how the sentence actually ended: ". . . while you're still young and have a pretty face."

For now, let's ignore the ageism, sexism, and general assholery of the comment. What stuck was this same old backhanded compliment I've received throughout my life. For me, "You have a pretty face" has always meant "You're a fat ass." Maybe I interpret it this way because I've spent most of my life living in one of three body types: slightly chubby, average chubby, and flirting-with-obese, extra chubby. There's something about a woman's fatness, especially if she's blessed with a symmetrical face, but even more especially if she's an olive-complected Latina who both summer-tans and winter-whitens nicely, that induces folks to comment frequently on her face. Saying to a chubby woman, "You have a pretty face," is asking for her to respond, "Aw, thanks for ignoring my disgusting body!" But I've never had the guts to reply that way, and my failure to do so disappoints me more than any excess body weight ever could.

Back to the comment's assholery: what my friend was saying, what killed me, was *it doesn't matter what you write—just sell yourself.* The marketing-acumen aspect of writing sickened me even before the existence of social media, so you can imagine how I feel about it now. Besides, it was ludicrous to believe a pretty headshot could help sell my book, though it's a moot point now. I'm no longer young, and to top it off, I never finished the book my poet friend insisted I should. I sure showed her.

(2) When I was growing up, Lala's pet name for me was Enriquita. For much of my life I believed "Enriquita" was the Spanish translation for the word "slow," or "dummy." If I forgot how to say a particular word in Spanish, for instance, the only language in which Lala and I could communicate, she would tease me, "Enriquita!" It was decades before I learned the word was not a Spanish synonym for "estúpido," and that "Enriquita's" provenance was this: Enrique had been a boy with special needs in Lala's village growing up. I want to say I valiantly chastised Lala for her cruelty toward poor Enrique, but I doubt it. Ironically, this faulty memory of mine would provoke Lala to call me Enriquita now, were she still alive to do so. I'd like to

be the kind of person who considers more deliberately the Enriques of the world—who he was, how cruelty touched him, and kindness, what he feared and loved. Instead, I obsess over the Lalas: the alluring, vain, temperamental, whose primary wish for me was that I grow to be beautiful. Though she didn't need to wish for it; a *pajarito* had already chirped to her this prophecy. Oh yeah, that was another thing about Lala. Animals spoke to her, and she spoke back, and though no one else had ever observed this, I was supposed to accept this—all her claims—without question.

Shortly after I learned to print my name in every book we owned, I admitted I wanted to grow up to become a writer. This should not have surprised her since, with boundless brio, she told me all her life stories, both real and imagined. She shook her head, said, "*Oy Dios mío*, writers are ugly. Have you ever seen one on TV? But at least it's no *doctor*." Why was becoming a doctor so ill-considered? "Their learning is never over! Always new ideas about the body and mind. *Qué pesado, tanto* relearning. Things you thought were true for years now *basura*." At the time I didn't dream of challenging her on the miseries of lifelong learning. Only much later I wondered: What was wrong with continually learning and starting over and over again across a life? Wasn't that exciting, all the yet-to-be-knowns? Wasn't this the only way to keep life from becoming a big sack of boring?

Lala finally acquiesced to the writer idea, on one condition: someday I would write about her. The whole Enriquita revelation had me thinking about how one could live with and love someone for so long and literally not understand the words they say to you, what they mean, and I questioned to what degree our miscommunications big and small devalued our love. So I offer her and that question here, in these pages, with the backdrop of the New Orleans where she helped raise me.

(3) In the months after Hurricane Katrina tore through the Gulf Coast in 2005, our Baton Rouge neighborhood off the LSU lakes, and the city in general, saw an influx of stray dogs. One morning, my now-husband, Brock, took his usual ride around the lakes and a brindled, emaciated pit-boxer threw herself in front of his bike. She performed

her classic damsel-in-distress move we'd come to know and love—rolled over on her back, pawed the air, and licked her lips. What else could he do? Brock magnanimously rescued her. Because I'm also magnanimous, and since no one else would take her, I agreed we'd keep her. And because she'd struggled through adversity to get to us, because we wanted to pay homage to our beleaguered city, we named her Nola. One of her many lovable tics was the insanely jealous face she made when surrounded by female doggy beauty. Nola's resentment in the presence of female dogs transformed her head's composition. Her brown eyes morphed gray, her soft face hardened. She was a canine Medusa who looked into a mirror and turned her own damned self to stone; we called it her Nola Face. It was a trait, I came to realize, that mirrored my own.

Only my Nola Face wasn't directed toward cuter women. I made mine in the presence of anyone who exhibited some coveted talent. Why did *they* get to run, write, love better than *I* did? This fixation impeded my ability to be in the world, to learn and relearn in the ways necessary to become the runner/lover/writer I wished to be. How could I be myself while ruled by base jealousies? How would I write a book in which I was a partial subject, when I couldn't even face myself? I aspire to reframe the Nola Face: make it less like my jealous dog and more like the city of my birth.

Forgive me, dear reader, I lied. All of the above are true. Only the title of the game, and the premise for this essay, was a lie. I spent so much of my life lying to Lala and the rest of my family, being the person I thought they expected me to be, rather than being myself. I equated "good" or even "adequate" as anti-Brooke. This is my attempt to become the pro-Brooke that is the spirit of Nola Face. The face of my dog and my birth city and me. Maybe we'll play the game again later, and I promise to try to be more truthful.

CIELITO LINDO

If it was bedtime, I wasn't sleepy. At four, I had too many stories to tell myself. I'd recently received the best present of my life from Abuelo: a series of personalized books in which I was the main character. The best of the set was *My Birthday Land Adventure*, in which a birthday elf leads Brooke (*me!*) down Read Boulevard, my street in New Orleans, and into the fantastical Birthday Land, where he offers me a bouquet of marigolds, an opal ring, and other October-themed birthday gifts. The more Abuelo reads me this book, the more I'm convinced my New Orleans streets hide portals to other worlds. Bedtime is my chance to expound upon these stories. On this night, I'm thinking up where I might take the elf for *his* birthday adventure.

My grandmother Lala sees my beloved books as a betrayal of our language. *Qué carajo, why aren't these in Spanish!* My love for them is apostasy. (I still regret that whenever I write her, in order for both my reader and myself to better understand her, I'm forced to translate her speech into English, a language she refused to learn after emigrating from Ecuador in the 1960s.) This apostasy feeds the new narrative Lala fears most: once I start school, I'll forget all about her. I'll spend my days learning American caca instead of staying at Lala's while my mother works long hours as a secretary at a law firm downtown. I won't beg for weekend sleepovers at Lala's like I do now, I'll make *tonta* friends who speak that ridiculous *idioma*. What she doesn't know is the stories I tell myself at bedtime, in my head, are all in English. The betrayal has already begun.

Most nights Lala interrupts my secret stories to make me pray in Spanish, aloud, to her. And to God, I guess. Tonight, she's late, possibly catching up on her beloved telenovela, *Tú o Nadie*, filled with the *tracción* I'm not yet interested in, so I begin alone. *Padre Nuestro que estás en los cielos, santificado sea Tu Nombre.* It's funny when I consider my prayers in Spanish versus English. Spanish prayers feel more powerful because they're sanctioned by Lala, and even Diosito knows she's *una bruja.* A witch. She has the ability to make certain things happen. If someone has the hiccups, she'll sneak up from behind and smack a square of wet newspaper on their forehead—no more hiccups. She can cure any case of gas with a sprinkling of anise water and get rid of a stye by tying a piece of string into a bow around the middle finger on the opposite hand of the afflicted eye. Not to mention she can silence me like no one else by simply removing her *chancleta.* I wonder why we have to pray for things to happen when Lala can just do them and, also, whether Catholics are also allowed to be witches. Lala looms so large in both my reality and imagination that it seems like prayers, Dios Himself, and even the small spells I've seen her perform are all inventions to further tether us together.

For once, Lala's not here to oversee, so I relinquish *Padre Nuestro* to tell my own stories. I fall asleep planning a pool party for my birthday elf at the YMCA, a few blocks from Lala and Abuelo's house.

Suddenly Lala shakes me awake, puts my fingers in her mouth, and tells me, "If you don't sneak out with me to get some beignets, I'm going to chew these off one by one."

It's only a few moonlit interstate miles from Lala's home in New Orleans East to the French Quarter. I've only been awake for twenty minutes when Lala parks at the north end of the Quarter near the closed French Market. She drives a red Dodge Charger whose horn plays "La Cucaracha," solely, it seems, to humiliate me. Luckily, no one's around to hear her celebratory honk after finding free street parking. Summer nights like this one, the air moves in tandem with the Mississippi River, not a breeze, more like *un soplo de Dios.* God's breath. We're only a few steps into our beignet escapade when we come upon a statue of a man on a horse. The man wears armor, a crown of ivy, and he hoists a proud flag, shining golden in the moonlight. I ask Lala his name, and she tentatively reads the inscription: Joan of Arc. "This girl fought a war for New Orleans a long time ago, before even I was born. *Pero* . . . she also shaved her head. No good reason for any girl to do that."

Lala says she vaguely remembers learning about Joan of Arc in school but has forgotten most of her story. What matters is Joan was a rebel. Walking through my city way past bedtime, past a girl who shaved her head and fought and became a statue, I imagine I, too, could someday control my own destiny. I won't have to choose between Spanish and English, Lala or America, God or godlessness. I can be one with the streets of Orleans once rescued by a girl.

Shortly past Joan of Arc, there's a man lying on a bench. He's the statue's opposite, tucked tightly into himself, but his hair sticks out everywhere. I'm jealous he probably never has to wash it. His shirt slumps down off one shoulder, like someone recently grabbed it and flapped him about like Lala does with wet sheets before hanging them on the clothesline.

"Diosito asks us to love everybody," Lala tells me. "Except for *caras de verga.*" She knows I love it when she says dickface, so she uses the phrase whenever she can (and I admit, Spanish curses beat English ones almost every time). "But look, this guy seems nice. He has a cigarette!"

Lala bats her eyelashes, signals for the Marlboro tucked behind his ear. He hands it over, then pulls a matchbook from his socks, a quick magic trick, and lights it for her. His one open eye is sky blue, the color I covet over my dark brown, but that doesn't make up for his other eyelid, which appears to have been glued shut. I wonder if he can only see half the world. I remind myself to practice being one-eyed sometime.

Lala exhales like it's the first time she's ever breathed. "Thanks you, gentlemoon," she says. She introduces me. "This is Brooksita. *Mi hija.*" My daughter. It's not the first time she's pretended to be my mother in public, and like I respond to most of Lala's lies, I go with it.

"Be good to your mama," he tells me before rolling back into himself. I'd bet his eye could haunt me if I didn't listen, so I wouldn't dream of disobeying him. Even if he's technically wrong about the mama part.

The closer we get to Jackson Square, the greater the olfactory competition between horse shit on one side of Decatur and the sweet, fried dough on the other. Outside Café Du Monde, four Black street performers dressed in green candy cane–striped suits play guitars and trumpets and drums. A sign propped up behind a coin-filled hat reads their name: The Corner Band. Lala does a cumbia jig, which frankly doesn't fit with this music, as the hostess seats us at an outdoor table.

Despite clearly enjoying the band, Lala scoffs. "Those men don't love who they sing for, so they do it badly. Playing music like a conversation they've had so many times before, oh hello, how are you— *carajo*, they're sick of it."

All I can hear is the blow of the trumpet, the beat of the banjo. The men bob their heads up and down in perfect rhythm. This is American music, which I greatly prefer to Julio Iglesias and Luis Miguel, so I make sure not to insult her by bobbing my head too.

Pigeons cluster under the empty table next to us and feed on leftover beignet scraps.

"Did you know a *paloma* once flew onto my shoulder and kissed me on the cheek?"

"*No me burles*," I protest. "Birds can't kiss!"

"This one did. She pecked me right by my mole, trying to steal my beauty!" I make a dubious face, and she says, "*Te prometo*, you'll have that same beauty mark someday."

"No gracias, I don't want it."

"*Dios mío, Enriquita! Belleza es fuerza.*" Beauty is power.

"Anyway, why would a *bird* try to steal your *beauty*. Doesn't make sense."

"Who knows why anyone does what they do? Maybe because she was heartbroken. Because someone didn't love her back. I didn't force her to explain." She rolls her eyes as if this were the most obvious thing in the world.

"The bird didn't explain because birds can't talk."

"*Mija*, just because you never saw something doesn't mean it doesn't exist. Birds can talk, like people can fly right out of the cages they've been trapped in."

Lala uses this elliptical language, similar to children and drunks, that makes any subject of conversation sound like a fairy tale. Then again, from my earliest memories, she's spoken to me straightforwardly, as if I were her peer. Now she clarifies her cage metaphor: she's always felt trapped by men. It's a song I've heard before and will hear time and time again. Before I knew precisely what the word "rape" meant, I learned her first husband, Honesto, had raped her while they were dating, but since he'd stolen her virginity, she felt compelled to marry him anyway. In a different way, she felt trapped by her second husband, my abuelo, who didn't physically hurt her but abandoned her repeatedly for other women, only to return each time a contrite *hijo de su madre*. Over time I recognized Lala's beauty, which she'd so relied upon, had never been enough to save her, which later made me wonder: Why did she want beauty so badly for me?

For now, among the powdered sugar piled on deep-fried bread and café au lait, she tells me the *true* story of how she lost the beauty mark above her lip, the one that in pictures looks like a tiny, brown bubble. It used to live next to her left nostril, the place where she points for me to kiss and where there's a scar. The beauty-mark killer, she says, was Abuelo, who one night began kissing her face uncontrollably (when she was innocently standing there at the sink washing dishes, *imaginite!*). He started at her forehead and worked his way down. When he got to her mole he nibbled a little too hard, like a feeding bird, and tasted blood. The mole became infected and had to be removed. The moral here? "Any man or bird can rob your beauty at any time, so be prepared."

Sometime later, I'll hear another version of this story—this time, it was my mother who scratched off Lala's mole in a fit of jealousy (Mom never got the beauty mark Lala had promised her and thus made Lala pay for it). When Lala told the story this way, the moral was that beauty cannot be robbed; it is inherent, destined, and conquers even the most vicious jealousies. In her typical Lala vagary, depending on the context, she'll insist on the veracity of both versions. If she were alive right now to tell you her cause of death—congestive heart failure—she would, on the one hand, agree with the medical examiners: that at the age of eighty-four, years after giving up walking because it became too taxing, her heart no longer pumped blood through her body as well as it needed to, and it stopped working one morning while she slept. On the other hand, she'd swear the only plausible way to interpret congestive heart failure is that she died of a broken heart—because no one in her life (*me!*) had been able to love her sufficiently, so she finally gave up on utilizing her most essential muscle. I certainly don't know this yet at four years old, but it will become part of my life's mission to distinguish the reality of her stories from their fictions.

Post-beauty-mark story, she's in warning mode. "Your beauty will be a problem, because it will never be appreciated in this country. Because men will not know how to express their desires. En Ecuador, men sang to me as if it was their last song on earth, *con fuerza, con amor,* the way people did before they had language. All they say here is 'oh, you pretty.'" She twists up her lips, "'pretty,' *Dios mío, qué palabra tan fea.*" Such an ugly word.

"But wait," I say. "How could people sing without language?"

"*Mija,* you do too much asking-questions and not enough feeling-feelings."

To make up for the song I'll never hear from an American man, Lala sings me one of her favorites, "Cielito Lindo." The song reminds us how singing can make the heart happy. It's in the tradition of the French blazon, cataloguing the physical attributes of its subject: dark eyes, small mouth, beauty mark. In a few years, a dark mole will finally appear below the left corner of my lip. Lala will credit her frequent singing of these verses, along with her witchiness, for the magic that grew *ese lunar perfecto.* The perfect beauty mark. In one of the song's verses, when a bird abandons her nest and later finds it occupied by another, the moral is that she deserves to lose it. This line has always terrified me because I interpret it personally: if I ever left Lala's nest, could I be replaced? Where, then, would all that love go? But now, as back then, I can't shut off my mind from asking questions, while in my memory of this night, Lala performs all the feeling-feelings, singing the final verse that begs the listener to sing rather than cry: "Ay ay ay ay, / *Canta y no llores* . . ."

After we finish our beignets and café, we walk back down the street, Lala leading the way, with the sun not far behind, preparing to give us a new *cielito lindo*, a pretty sky. I don't remember seeing Joan of Arc again on this night, though when I walk past her these days, whenever I take my kids to visit my mother in New Orleans, I think of the only story Lala told me whose version never changed: how she watched her own mother die of tuberculosis at a TB camp where they were quarantined when Lala was only three years old. How blood poured from her mother's mouth like a river of chocolate. How her pharmacist father worked too much to take care of her, so Lala was sent to live with a gaggle of evil crone-aunts in Manta who instantly hated her beauty and childish mischief, who made her kneel on rice for their fun, who'd smack her face raw while she screamed, "Is somebody hitting me? I don't feel anything!," and who, oh yes, once shaved off her long, dark hair as punishment for some wildness or other. Back then, before I was born and gave her the name Lala, she was Gladys. This girl with the shaved head would grow up not to rescue New Orleans streets but instead gift them to me.

And suddenly, I'm in bed again. I remember nearly everything about that night, but not arriving back at our car or driving the 1-10 back to Lala's house on Michoud Boulevard. Lala had the power to magically place me into the French Quarter and then back home. Tucking me in, she says, "This was all for you, *todo es para ti*."

Before Lala begins our prayers, I say a private one in my head, another *secreto* I keep from her every night. I press my hands together in supplication, fingers pointed to the ceiling (so the prayers go straight to heaven). I understand secret prayers are more like wishes, and to involve God in wish fulfillment, if He exists, means they likely won't come true. So far they haven't anyway. I've secretly prayed for invisibility, for overnight adulthood, for lighter skin and blue eyes. Maybe the problem all along was that my secret, internal prayers were in English. My prayer tonight may be my most insidious yet, but it's the one I most desperately desire. Only much later will I understand the depths of its irony: my secret prayer, in Spanish, is that I'll be able to take Lala into the world of English with me. Sort of like I'd been planning to do with the birthday elf, except with the stakes much higher, because this is real life. I can convert her, make her slightly more normal, more American, more like me. I pray for power over her. *Mi fuerza.* But without the beauty part.

Then, Lala begins our real, Spanish prayers as we always do: first by blessing the universe and then working our way down to our community, our family, ourselves.

"*Que Dios bendiga a todos en el mundo que sufren, los que tienen nada, los que roban lo mismo que los que fueron robado.*" It was important to start with the great sufferers of the world—the hungry, the thieving, the lonely. Those who didn't have bread or Lala to comfort them, like I did.

"*Que Dios bendiga la familia.*"

"*Los que siguen en Ecuador.*"

"*Y Abuelo. Mama y Papa.*"

"*Tú y yo.*"

"And God bless the French Quarter man who gave you a cigarette. Even though you shouldn't smoke."

She reminds me, "*En español, cielito.*"

Until now, writing these memories down, I've forgotten that one of Lala's dearest names for me, *cielito*, means not just "little sky" or "pretty sky" but also "my darling," and "little heaven." As far as Lala was concerned, I was all of these at once. Boundless. That's a lot to live up to. Maybe that's why, at four, I'm praying for another version of life I can't even imagine, saying yes to it, and saying no (or *not quite*) to the life she's given me so far. Even if it means the nest of her heart might later be inhabited by someone else. In my secret prayer, I'm taking the chance of being *cielito* to no one.

This night, like all the others, we begin and end in the first language I ever spoke. With Lala gone for years now, I can barely remember how to mouth the Spanish words I so loved, the curses, the sobriquets. It's felt like a betrayal in my writing to translate Lala from Spanish to English, and now I'm thinking about how translation betrays the younger me too. In Spanish, I saw my city's streets, I learned to yearn, to doubt, and to believe. I learned to love her and be loved in return, imperfectly, profoundly, with a depth some lonely people— *los que sufren*—might even pray for. But some words require no translation; they're the same in both languages. Together Lala and I say aloud our final words to each other every night: *Amen.*

THREE SACRAMENTS

I'm nine years old the day my mother dies and comes back to life and, if I ever believed at all, it's the day I give up on Christ.

You might expect the reverse—the hope for miracles, the power of prayer—but when I make my final judgment, I don't know yet, and won't know for a long time that she has died and returned. All I'm told is Mom's having pregnancy complications. The baby, my would-be half-sister, is gestating at twenty-three weeks and must be delivered dangerously early. Everyone waits and prays. Doctors work and pray. At school, my teacher's hand on my shoulder a few seconds too long in that comforting way, her eyes say: I'll pray for you. Before bed I press my hands into a teepee and try earnestly at first then only pretend to pray.

My mother's death-day memory, she recalls later, is the moment when according to scripture, she might have seen the light, though here the primary sense was smell: a priest with severe halitosis read her last rites. As he anointed her forehead, slanting into his Latin, she thought right before the line went flat: *to hell with this, I've got to live, I can't die breathing this stench.* Years after, these ninety seconds during which she no longer technically exists, when there is space for our collective levity, we call this sentiment grace.

PENANCE

Because Mom is in the hospital, my confirmation must be postponed. My parents divorced soon after I was baptized, one sacrament built upon the dissolution of the matrimonial other. It's a cursory, Mardi Gras type of Catholicism practiced in my family and most others I know: everyone says they believe and sometimes attend Mass, but mostly they drink to all that. My father, a nonbeliever, spurns chalice for tumbler, Bible for Bellow.

I suspect my stay with him during my mother's illness might be penance for a past I have yet to (then or now) fully piece together. I know he scared me once when, drink sloshing in one hand and trapped mouse in another, he swung the rodent by its toothpick tail, insisted what was dead couldn't hurt me. And I've heard the story from before I had a memory, the one about my parents' marriage being over: during a fight, he said *fuck the baby*, and the baby was me. But there is so much I can't fathom, and I don't expect God or my father to reveal any of it. I've teepee'd my hands. I've tried.

These nights, motherless at my father's, I listen for skittering mice, wishing them dead. My books aren't here, but my Grandma Connie's dusty red Bible sits there on the nightstand, serving not as reading material but as proof of itself. The main character, Jesus, was a child once too, according to Luke, who ran away from his parents to preach in the temple. That's the difference between me and Jesus: he gets annoyed because he understands what no one else can, while I rage because I understand nothing. It's why I can't get into the Bible, or Jesus as a character. Sure, he's endlessly kind and loving, that's great, but he knows too much and knows he knows. I fall asleep with my hands in their skyward position, all I can offer.

Later that night, the ringing phone wakes me. Its loud ping on the receiver. My father's cry from the next room.

CONFIRMATION

In this Gentilly Woods home (which, decades later, will be gutted by the hurricane some 700 Club holies said God had decreed for our city's sins), in the moment I don't yet know my mother is dying across the river at St. Luke's, while my father's words float through the slatted panel doors separating our rooms that too closely resemble a confessional screen, I silently watch him.

His skin smell is everywhere, bourbon and unctuousness. He tears his hair. The tumbler clinks hard against his teeth, but he doesn't notice. He spills. My fingers pull at the slats. He weeps as if atop the Mount of Olives a different sort of sermon: God has fucked him over, God sucks, God doesn't really exist, but in case He does, He better bring her back. Through the slats I see his form cut horizontally in half, and watching him cry, I can't know what I don't know. That a tragedy has occurred, and that it will be sublimated by a miracle. I can't remember if another call soon followed, if or when his cry became joyous. I know only what I see, both then and now, in that second of my memory: my father praying. My father desperate, breathless in love.

Within the confines of the Catholic Church, I'm never confirmed. When the time comes, I'll skip the classes, lean into the side of the old stone church with a boy, allow both sides of my favorite Sunday school verb: to receive and to be received. Only now, long after my mother's resurrection, and after our city's flood, do I pinpoint my moment of confirmation: my father crying over my mother, his sacrificial prayer so far beyond all my teepees, his worship for her exceeding anything he'd feel for literature or other lovers or even me. For her, I saw, he would kneel and beg and believe. In fear of what I don't know and what I do, I'd like to touch his cheek, pray together so piously it might spring some faith, offer ablutions with our tears. Yet I don't open the door. Instead I ache remotely, like him, to someday find and create my own miracle of a love that never dies. In that way I've remained confirmed.

PIPÓN

Pipón came to us by air—ten hours from Quito to New Orleans International, a porkpie-hatted, five-foot, stuffed clown seated on Abuelo's lap. Had my grandfather enjoyed small talk, had an earnest seatmate noted that such an enormous clown must have been reserved for someone so small, that perhaps congratulations were in order this *Feliz Navidad*, Abuelo would've replied with a terse *sí* to end conversation. Years before, Abuelo had come to Los Estados Unidos by sea to open Selbor Supplies—a decidedly Anglo-sounding name that might have repulsed Lala, had it not been their own surname, Robles, spelled backward—as a ship chandler in the Port of New Orleans. So Abuelo and Pipón traveled separately, then together, cutting a path up the belly of the world to mold a part-here, part-there me.

Pipón traversed hemispheres to be my first recorded gift: twelve pounds, red-nosed, felt-vested, white-gloved. Named after his pot belly, *panzón*. He even came with a nursery rhyme, one I thought for years we'd written, inspired by and sung daily for him, part of the soundtrack of my childhood. But we invent nothing: the song is of archaic Latin American, though not necessarily Ecuadorian, origin, a didactic children's song intended to instill good behavior with Pipón as the preeminent model. He is introduced as handsome and clean, a prolific hand washer.

> *Pipón es un muñeco, muy guapo y de cartón.*
> *Se lava las manitos, con agua y con jabón.*

There he is, leaning over one of my early smiles, reflecting his own, while I tummy-time on the bed, neither of us aware we're posing. There he is again, standing alone in the middle of the hallway in my memory, not in his steady position in my bedroom corner. Lala's hiding from us, I later learn, on the other side of the wall. Me, I'm barely breathing, believing in the miracle of, finally, my anthropomorphized toy companion walking toward me, and I run up to embrace him with an *oy, Pipón*, but he falls over with my touch. Lala appears at the end of the hallway and asks what the hell is wrong with me—why aren't I *asustada* by her trick? And when I cry for the lost miracle I thought I'd seen, Lala throws up her arms, thinks this is a fit. She reminds me Pipón wouldn't act that way—he doesn't even cry when the comb tears out his hair. She tells me: you don't know what hurt is yet.

Cuando se peina el pelo con peines de marfil.
Cuando se da tirones no llora ni hace así.

But can you believe that, as years passed, I flung Pipón to the ground from his bedroom-corner perch, floating my body atop his, too old to think so but knowing anyway that he felt me, and my heft pressing him down meant I was present, alive for now, and symbiotically I inspired his ever-present smile, so when nightly I prayed for everyone's life as Lala instructed (since our lives could end *cualquier segundo*, especially hers), more than anything I was grateful that he understood my currently alive-but-someday-dead daily grief as no one else could, because one of the reasons on many nights I was finally able to go to sleep—that complete capitulation so closely resembling death—was that he lay next to me in bed, and I knew then he was creased and stuffed and sewn and flown straight up the globe just for me, and that unlike a pet, and any person I'd ever love, and me, he'd never die.

Cuando las estrellitas empiezan a lucir.
Pipón se va a la cama y se acuesta a dormir.

But if you believe in Pipón, and he's in your growing world, and he takes up so much space (though not enough to crowd your late Abuelo's absence, which makes the *muñeco's* static smile, and Lala's inducement that prayer relieves suffering, even more of a lie), he's someone you'll eventually have to introduce to people. How do you say, puberty-monstered and bleeding and raw: this is my five-foot clown, Pipón? *Oy*, and that name: a reminder of my otherness, part brown part whiteness, therefore what am I, hence my unbelonging, hence my unlovability. Funny how quickly we slide there as children, maybe even as adults. Or maybe it was me.

Cuando le dan la sopa, no ensucia el delantal,
pues come con cuidado, parece un collegial.

When no one, especially not Pipón (who by this point had become, in my more cynical moments, merely an uppity "good guy" clown), could understand me, nor I them, this dankest warmth I began to crave: a neighborhood boy who openly admired my breasts at thirteen. The oversized doll was *ridic*, said the boy, who rejected any hint of my sentimentality or autobiography—it was as if we were each of us created in the moments before we met, and the only relevant story was the one happening now. We'll be fucking soon, he announced, and I felt lucky to be marked by him, so when he and a group of his friends kidnapped Pipón from my room, taking him out to the street on their Schwinns, launching him into the air and catching him one armed, with the coolness and fluidity fourteen-year-old boys, then, seemed born with, and dropped him finally when their arms got tired, called him a fat fuck, rolled over his head, simulated an ass raping, knifed and widened a hole in one of his seams, cutting a path down his belly from north to south to reveal the inner world of him, mounds and mounds of diaphanous white gauze, more of it than I ever could've imagined, floating down the street into neighbor's front yards, while I watched from behind the screen door at Pipón's tortured unbecoming . . . well, I wish I could say now that I'd done something. Or said it. I'd cry later, much later I'd cry the river of tears where I'd settle my new country of Female-Hurt Land, days and months of tears over the whims of this boy and others, what their hands and arms could do, but at that crucial moment I only feigned anxiety, made it a reason to call them out as fuckers, feared mostly the nuisance of hiding a five-foot broken no-longer-*muñeco* from Lala.

I certainly didn't consider the last verse of Pipón's song—

Pipón dame la mano, dame un buen apretón.
Que quiero ser tu amigo, Pipón, Pipón, Pipón!

—that Pipón's whole reason for being was friendship, for you to hold his hand and tell the truth, simple and small—here I am, I'm yours— but I thought of this later, and how Pipón died alone, like the rest of us, and how, like a lot of loves I lose, I wished I could remeet him for the first time, knowing then what I know now, and love him better for that, though of course I conceived none of this when, tenderloined and new, learning to smile, and mean it, that first Christmas in pictures, Pipón came to us by air.

WHAT I KNOW ABOUT THE CHICKEN LADY

Once, days or hours after a woman had died in her apartment on Tchoupitoulas, the Chicken Lady gently tore the yellow police tape off the door's threshold and led my father inside without a word about it. My father doesn't know, as I don't, if the Chicken Lady killed that woman all those years ago or if the Chicken Lady herself is still alive today. I don't know which parts of her are my father's fantasy for a past long gone, a past entirely without me. I don't know if she loved him, but I do know my father, parts of him, and I know he doesn't believe in magic, or God, but he believes in the Chicken Lady.

I learned this part once in my twenties when he invited me over for lunch, his euphemism for drinks. By this time, Hurricane Katrina had washed him away to Baker, Louisiana, ninety miles northwest of New Orleans, the city where he helped raise me every other weekend during the first decade of my life. In the next decade, he began disappearing for months, then years, at a time. He called in 1997 after no word since Christmas of '95. He had a hilarious story to tell me: *I got shot at the Friendly Inn!* The irony, right? Wasn't that absurd? When I expressed alarm, asked why this happened, he brushed off the foolish concern: This went down months ago between people who were now in jail, and when I said it was a miracle he wasn't hit, he said, *no, it's that the guy who shot me was the most imbecilic fuck who ever lived.* Then, as now, I took what I could get; his stories and their perverse logic implied whatever he offered was more than enough. Because it was.

Now as an adult in my thirties, he's invited me over for lunch several times. But I've actually eaten at his shotgun house twice. The first time, he offered a handful of pistachios and a slice of Swiss; the second, half a square of Domino's thin crust pepperoni. Afterward I'd lied that I was full, and that it was delicious. On these dates, though, we've drunk close to our weight in rum and Coke or beer or Boone's Farm. If he's thirsty before noon, so am I.

Each lunch after the first pour, my father pats his stomach and reports his weight: last time he was down to 159. I'm supposed to be proud, and I know this because he asks if I am. I also know never to try to lead in this dance of conversation, even if I want to, that he will reveal only what he feels like revealing, that I should tread lightly with questions, and while discussing what we're reading or binge watching is highly encouraged, I should never mention writing. He was a writer, though he gave up on that somewhere near the time he once told me he gave up on love. I used to know the date before I began writing myself, but now, because of our tacit concern he might become material, I'm scared to ask.

My visits are an excuse for him to narrate the stories he might've written. He, the purveyor of words, and I, the passive listener. Once my father is drunk, he speaks in all caps, but when he's working his way there, it's italics.

She lived across from Tipitina's where she tended bar when we weren't high. Most beautiful Black woman I'd ever seen. Thing was I never saw her hair, do-rag always covering it up. During the week I worked some stupid ass job holding up a neon sandwich board outside Radio Shack, and I ate two 7–11 hot dogs per day, that was it. Rest of my money I saved for weekends with the Chicken Lady. Once we smoked two hundreds' worth. And I kept doing it, her and the crack, but then it stopped working. She kept trying to fix me. One time buck-ass naked she hovered over me and went, "Roy, I'ma do something special for you—it's the thing I did to the Chicken Man before he died."

"What did she do?" I ask.

Doesn't matter, didn't work. Falling in love again, finding joy, seemed hilarious. So after we did our thing and nothing worked she went,

What I Know about the Chicken Lady   27

"Roy, I'ma make it so you never want for a woman again. I'ma make you an amulet." Now, I didn't fall for her voodoo shit but I had twenty bucks left over so I thought it's either this amulet or more crack. And I'd never had an amulet.

I watched from bed while she mashed up all kinds of crazy shit in her kitchen. She went, "I need a pair of moth's wings . . . some navel lint . . . a piece of that crack rock." I was like, okay, Chicken Lady. She scratched under her do-rag and pulled out one thick hair to tie it all together. When she was done she slid it in my pocket and went, "Keep this with you. You'll never want again."

Next four weeks, swear to God, I couldn't get rid of women. On the bus in midtown I'd see one from way back, broad from high school, and she'd look me up and down. Invite me over. Day later a girl from the old neighborhood, or my ex-girlfriend's friend looking for a revenge fuck, would sidle up all crazy-eyed. For a whole month I ran into every woman who'd ever wanted to sleep with me. Most of them probably never wanted to, but I'm telling you, it was that amulet that made them do it.

"So you believe in voodoo now?"

Not any more than I believe in Jesus Christ, but I'm telling you, this shit worked. Worked so good I hated it, threw the amulet down the sewer on Canal. Let the rats fuck each other instead.

"When was this? What happened to the Chicken Lady?"

Aaaah, I don't know. Look, I don't like to talk about those days.

Maybe because I've asked too many questions the spell is broken. My father's stories of his hiatus from my life too often unspool like a glorious do-rag till, abruptly, they stop half unwound. In his presence, despite being presumably grown-up and whole, I still *want* too much, meaning both lack and desire. Who were you when I was fifteen, twenty-four, thirty, what else did you see and do? I want to ask. *More*, I want to threaten.

But I don't. Instead, I take the Chicken Lady when I can get her.

There, in our silent sipping, I want her, instead: *teach me to make an amulet*. To create the power to force his words into me, to force mine into him, to give me back—if not time, if not a form, finally, for years of abiding, stoppered daughter's love—then more stories. More

What I Know about the Chicken Lady

Chicken Lady and more everything else I don't know. She, concocting the ideal set of ingredients. Dad and I, then, storying without end.

Lacking her, just me and Dad on his porch, I consider what I'd have to work with here to make an amulet: his cigarette dregs, aluminum can tabs, fleas that appear sometimes on his white socks, then disappear. I could collect these ingredients and take them home with me where I'll write this shard of his story, combine and crush them all together, adding to them with the temerity of a Chicken Lady, a period at the end of one of my sentences.

McCLEANING WITH THE DUSTBUSTER

My mother twice bought a salesman's door-knock pitch, and both investments were, in one way or another, a response to one of her failed marriages. The first pitch came from David Vitter, chinless Republican candidate for the Louisiana House of Representatives from the Eighty-First District, running on the chinless platform of family values. His was a good ole, traditional campaign, knocking on constituents' doors and appealing to their needs and concerns for the future. My mother invited him into our dustbusted living room. My father had been a radical Vietnam/Watergate leftist, lying across Robert E. Lee Boulevard in New Orleans to protest the draft, kicking over the TV during Nixon's "I'm not a crook" telecast. After several years of marriage, his behaviors lost whatever charm they once possessed. When Vitter arrived at our door in 1992, my parents had been divorced for eight years. For my father, politics was sacrosanct, and supporting a Republican was anathema to everything he believed to be good and true. It was perhaps on this ground alone Mom promised Vitter he could count on her vote.

Soon afterward, another salesman introduced her to the exorbitant Tri-Star vacuum cleaner, a silver, futuristic-looking contraption with a long hose separating the motor from the power brush. The Tri-Star promised everything: healthier environment, enhanced home appearance, peace of mind. My mother was finalizing her second divorce—she required some sense of "here is something I will never have to think about again." The Tri-Star, purchased around the time

Vitter was sworn into the state legislature, has lived through more than a dozen political cycles, including the public admission by Vitter in 2007 that for years he'd habitually solicited D.C. prostitutes. His wife, Wendy, joined him in solidarity at the press conference. Hands clasped at her front, she wore a form-fitting leopard print dress while her husband repeatedly asked her, his constituents, and God for their collective forgiveness. She, of course, said nothing. They remain married today.

My mother handed down that Tri-Star vacuum cleaner to me after my wedding. The vacuum bears some resemblance to the robot Johnny 5 from the film *Short Circuit* and is about as ambulatory as Steve Guttenberg is funny. Sometimes I wonder if its lugubriousness is worth its power. There's no corner or closet roomy enough to fit it.

For now, though, the Tri-Star is doing its job. Seven years later, I remain married to my husband, breaking my mother's record for her first two marriages.

My writing desk is hella dusty. Noticing this calls to mind a foremost precept of cleaning: dust accumulates most quickly in unused spaces. Thus, I am not writing enough. If I wrote more, the dust might fall more heavily upon the nightstand, on the oscillating fan, on the sewing machine in the corner of my office that I never use, sewing having always been my mother's (never mine) one domestic delight. She'd hoped to pass onto me the meditative practice of needle-and-threading what was easily reparable. Tighten holes, widen seams, close the gaps. Still, she's proud I grew up with zero domestic proclivities. She's joked that no woman should feel compelled to sew or cook or toil over any other household chore, for that matter—they should divorce if it came to that.

Dusting is the minutiae of moving objects around. So is marriage and, sometimes, so is divorce.

Carried by these musings, I bump my silver philodendron too forcefully with my dust rag—its soil dumps neatly into the small cubic space between my writing desk and bookshelf. The Tri-Star's hose attachment is broken, and I can't sweep away the wet soil lest it grind into the carpet. If only an appliance existed, I consider, that will pick up just this dirt, in just this small space.

I had forgotten all about the Dustbuster. For children of the eighties, dustbusting was an invigorating verb. After dinner it was my job to dustbust the crumbs from the table and sometimes, gleefully, from my little sisters' shirtfronts. Through easy tasks like dustbusting we learned the virtues of responsibility and cleanliness, in the Mc sort of way. My eighties were filled with Mc-food (frozen or fast), Mc-parents (stepfathers), and Mc-neighborhoods (subdivisions built up in a few weeks with the same three house plans multiplied endlessly down the block). Mcs were shoddy replacements for the real thing.

One sixth-grade summer afternoon I attempted a cleaning shortcut: rather than vacuuming the living room, as I'd been tasked, I resolved to dustbust every inch of its twist pile carpet in long, straight lines. But the Dustbuster clogged on my third row, and it died on the fourth. To clean it out, I detached the nozzle from the handle and spilled crumbs everywhere, for which I reluctantly lugged out the Tri-Star.

The Dustbuster was invented in 1979, the same year as the McDonald's Happy Meal, and a year after that, both the Chicken McNugget and I were born. Carroll Gantz, Black & Decker's Industrial Design manager, marketed the Dustbuster as a portable suction device for picking up light dirt and debris. But that was the thing: it didn't do much else. It sucked the surface grime but couldn't penetrate to the root. In the eighties I knew, McDonald's Mc-fed and the Dustbuster Mc-cleaned.

The original Dustbuster was a cream-colored plastic duckbill with a single brown button to rev its tiny motor. To charge one meant matching it up to its opposite-shaped wall holder. It looked like two hands clasping together. Like a prayer.

Our Dustbuster hung next to my mother's wood carving of the Serenity Prayer, which seemed the most permanent thing in our house by virtue of its basically being a letter to God—*God, grant me the serenity to accept what I cannot change*—though I never heard Mom ask God to grant her a thing. During one of her fights with my stepfather, the prayer was knocked from the wall. Once rehung, the carving remained askew on the wall for a long time, a rearrangement I thought most appropriate.

Were my mother's remarriages what Samuel Johnson called "the triumph of hope over experience"? Or, ultimately, the failure of equitable delegation? Promises weren't made only at the end of a church aisle, I intuited. A couple's foundation wasn't so simple as "man and wife," and the sickness and health and love and death weren't even the half of it. Often before those bigger tests played out, a couple lived together, slowly aged together, moved around in lockstep or with four left feet, depending on the day. And rather than acceding to the inequitable dynamic of our very first relationships, those between parents and children, a married couple made their own rules. Cultivated a day-to-day routine endowing each with specific parts to play. Both of my stepfathers were natural tinkerers, so they would be our home's occasional handyman—cleaning gutters, repairing the garbage disposal—performing tasks inconceivable for my idealist father who was versed in the oeuvre of Graham Greene but couldn't hang a picture frame. And my mother, in her second-wave feminist dream that women could do anything and have it all, reflexively took up the mantle of "if you do the tinkering, I'll take care of everything else! I'll dust and cook and clean and work full time and do pretty much all the kid stuff and still love you unconditionally, because I'm that strong and powerful!" In other words, rather than balancing their duties or at least having a conversation about them that might allow for future fluidity, it was: mother = everything, Mc-father = whatever he's in the mood for.

At some point, probably when the burden of her ceaseless domestic drudgery began outweighing her husband's facility with a screwdriver, or how hilarious he could be when drunk or stoned, my mother's purview on their respective roles sharpened. Both my Mc-parents, for example, were in the beginning described by my mother as real men's men: handy, diffident, fun. After a few years they were selfish drunks, that last word always an uppercut—there was nothing more to say or think about who they were. That lovely marriage pronoun, the *we*, was gone. Each spoken *I* became a towering, dauntless god, while the *you* was a stub of the toe, a malignant growth. Marriage became a war with clearly defined sides, and as with most warring parties, each side saw itself as the war's victim and hero.

During my adolescence, while my mother gradually fell out of sync with her second marriage, she became enamored with an epigram of unknown origin, pithy and reductive enough to sound to my young ears like premonitory advice: "Men may work from sun to sun, but women's work is never done." The couplet became such a popular refrain for her that, in seeming solidarity, my first Mc-father occasionally parroted it as well, letting us all know he, too, was aware of its truth. Men, in effect, have a sole job in a marriage, while women own all of them. To me the phrase sounded dirty coming from him, a prolix alternative to the beautiful brevity of "thank you." But it was even more cringeworthy coming from her, akin to an "it is what it is" shoulder shrug. Why did she accept a position within her own home that drove her crazy? Was it the married woman's fate to passive-aggressively, ineffectually complain? Was every marriage doomed to stasis until at some point both partners tacitly agreed to stop working on it altogether?

Here's how, in each of my mother's marriages, the stopping started: more and more frequently after one of their fights, when words were no longer sufficient to communicate their disgust—his hands on her throat, her nails in his cheeks, each sound and scene a rolling pin across my insides—the most interminable sound became their protracted silence. Weeks without acknowledgment of each other, ghost parents floating around the house. The standard emotional cleanup following a fight—the *I'm sorry honeys* and *never agains*—regressed to a spit-and-shine job at best, hardly even Dustbuster-worthy. Eventually, every ignored resentment piled too high and deep for anyone to tackle. Betrayal and fear shoved into every closet, mutual antipathy ground down into every thread of our twist-pile carpet. I wanted to dustbust the marriage detritus, dustbust her justifications, but I'd already learned: the Dustbuster can only hold so much.

In my marriage I've broken all the rules I made for myself as a child: *I'll never yell, he'll never drink too much, we'll never spout shit we can't take back*, we'll love just enough to forever keep us in an orderly, perfect alignment. I didn't know then that getting dirty isn't a choice. For us, it's been inevitable.

In our marriage, we fight. In some of our fights, my past is transmogrified. We get mad, we ruin dinner, I break a remote, throw a phone, he slams a door, punches the wall, I fling myself off the porch and scream into the grass. Yet the difference is the aftermath: that incontrovertible grime it leaves behind that we willfully, immediately recognize, and labor at once to scrub away. Rather than allowing our bitterness to slowly boil then optimistically evaporate with time, mirroring the fights I was bred on, we call out the other's mess when we see it. With every *why* and *what for* and *please can we not anymore* and *what did you mean*, we wipe down the obvious films of dust and move on to where decay resides: those concealed psychic baseboards and window panes, the forgotten space behind the toilet. We take on this grit together to see clearly where it is we live, and with whom. It is not in a carving on the wall but in this work where we find our prayers, and help each other answer them.

Still, despite these ideals, in my marriage I've spent more time than I'd like to admit parsing out whose mess is whose. Sure, I'm happy to wipe down my desk in my office, but when my husband announces our dining room table looks dusty, I ask, "Does it?" and give him a look, wait for him to clean it. The longer I'm married, though, the more I wonder who is delineating the *his* role and the *hers*. It's difficult to unlearn what our childhoods have encoded, what we never believed but enacted for the families who would accept nothing else, because we were playing the parts they'd prescribed. According to my mother, I should grow up to never take shit from men, let them clean up their own messes. According to my Mc-fathers, I should become the kind of woman who doesn't give men so much shit. It is through the continual polishing of my relationship that I've been able to gradually reject that either/or dichotomy. The more time we spend dusting ourselves off after a fight, or spot cleaning our marriage when we're not, the more the influence of Mc-everythings from the past starts to subside. Because there is no precedent for the scene in which I often find myself: my husband in our kitchen, mixing sauces for Chicken Mario or a red pepper and tofu stir-fry, working purposefully toward each meal that feeds us fully. We rarely eat from the paper sacks of my youth. For an aesthetic sense of parallelism, and as a gesture of gratitude, I make sure we eat his lovely dinners on my shiny tables. No: *our* dinners, *our* tables.

When the Smithsonian acquired an original model of the Dustbuster in 1995, the year my mother began her third marriage, 100 million had been sold. McDonald's, meanwhile, heavily marketed the Arch Deluxe sandwich in an effort to cultivate a more adult image. Only no one bought it. It was a standard burger with all the regular fixings, but with the lagniappe of sweet Spanish onions and, as noted in one advertisement, "a secret sauce for grown-ups." The problem, it seemed, was the tremendous effort and dollars spent in the narrow hope of catering to adults. Millions of sesame seeds atop their potato flour buns went uneaten, went unspilled upon the twist-pile carpeted floors of America, went un-dustbusted. McDonald's experiment with maturity resulted in one of the most expensive flops in the history of branding.

Black and Decker now sells nine popular models of the personal vacuum that pivot easily to pick up larger debris, use lithium-ion technology powered by cyclonic action, offer a more hygienic cleanup with less clogging than ever before. The world apparently still needs the Dustbuster, but I don't. When I spill plant soil on the carpet I vow to get the old Tri-Star repaired. I'll accept no substitutes if we're going to go all the way, because a real partnership calls for a real vacuum. In our marriage, for better or worse, my husband does the cooking. We share the cleaning.

LYING IN TRANSLATION

If you decided to leave Nola for good, for work or change of scenery or love, as I did in the aughts, you'd probably want to stop for gas and snacks before following the pine-framed highway of I-10 East. These days you wouldn't veer off on Michoud Boulevard, one of the city's last exits, since there's so little there. Plus, potholes every few yards will fuck up your tires with a quickness. But back in the day, if you yearned for escape, as I often did in the eighties and nineties, you might take Michoud and loop back under the overpass for a last stop at Schwegmann's or Exxon. Whatever shop you entered in that New Orleans East neighborhood, you'd likely step into a place where throughout my childhood, my grandmother stole, and I lied. This was the rhythm of our days: in the English-speaking world where Americans chirped *ese maldito inglés*, she spoke Spanish, and I served as translator.

I learned to lie well. Because at the TG&Y off Michoud, for example, Lala deigned to purchase household items like toilet paper or detergent but pocketed any small toy I desired. Then in the checkout line, if the cashier asked how we were doing, Lala would smilingly reply in Spanish with something like, "I'm stealing from you, dumbass." Those poor cashiers thought our routine so cute: the Hispanic woman and the granddaughter who spoke for her. That nice lady who complimented their haircuts or the store's cleanliness. The woman who, no matter what foreign sounds came from her mouth, was, as translated by her companion, always having a lovely day.

Lying in translation was the definitive marker of my childhood. No way could I tell the world the truth about who Lala was. At home she was my world, and I hers—*mi amor, mi vida, mi cielito lindo*—but publicly she made me cringe, with her loud talking and incessant jokes at the expense of the gringo suckers. She seemed to believe that because she spoke in a language those gringos didn't understand, they couldn't see or hear her either.

With the exception of her black leather *Biblia*, she was generally antibook; reading was the singular thing, other than Lala, that made my world go round. Thus, I came to identify Spanish with fierce love and anti-intellectualism, and English with people who created stories that lasted. The older I grew, the more confusing this became, since Lala ruled my life in Spanish, but from my limited perspective, English ruled the printed world I'd woven through my life. So who was really in charge here? For the time, I exalted one character, one *presidenta*, one god. Lala.

My initial defection from Spanish occurred when I was ten years old. At that time, two things happened concurrently that caused Lala to look at me in a way she never had before, with mild detachment: my mother gave birth prematurely to my youngest sister Alexa, and in the process, they both nearly died. Doctors (in English) and Catholic priests (in Spanish) declared their survivals a miracle, though I was carted off to stay with my father, so I experienced none of this firsthand. For a long time I translated the holy trinity of their suffering—Mom's, Alexa's, Lala's—as primarily a story I was excluded from. Yet as Alexa became Lala's *milagro* and even her *cielito* (*my* name, *my* position), I didn't resent my baby sister. Like a writer, like a human, I created a narrative to fit my current needs: my family was rebuilding itself after trauma, and I was outside of it, out of the way, where I belonged, nose in a book, eyes occasionally peering over in case I was needed. But I wasn't. Most of those weeks with my father are smudges in my memory; more vivid were the written worlds of Ann M. Martin and Wilson Rawls. Without my act of reading, the worlds contained within those books did not exist. Books needed me to make them real. My family did not. So I matched my face to Lala's—mildly detached, but curious, observant to the life going on around me to which I felt I had little access.

This is also around the time when I mostly stopped thinking in Spanish, thus stopped feeling as much in the language. This required a sort of double-translation, meaning I had to translate Lala's words and deeds not only to others, but to myself, in the primarily English life I was living. Translating these memories and Lala's actions back into English now—back to you—becomes then a triple-translation, diced up by time, language, and memory, so no matter how honest I try to be, it feels false.

In considering this false feeling, I'm reminded of a moment in Richard Rodriguez's memoir *Hunger of Memory*, when as a boy, a white friend asks him to translate what Rodriguez's Mexican grandmother has yelled out to him from her window: "[My friend] wanted to know what she had said. I started to tell him—to translate her Spanish words into English. The problem was, however, that though I knew how to translate exactly *what* she had told me, I realized that any translation would distort the deepest meaning of her message: It had been directed only to me. This message of intimacy could never be translated because it was not *in* the words she had used but passed *through* them. So any translation would have seemed wrong; her words would have been stripped of any essential meaning. Finally, I decided not to tell my friend anything. I told him that I didn't hear all she had said."

Rodriguez expresses here the untranslatability not only of language but of people and their intimacies. I feel already the person I've sketched so far is more Ecuadorian imp than Lala herself. How to capture her generosity followed by her startling moments of pettiness, the great love she proffered, then at turns withheld, without having you hear her voice directly? How do I stop you from taking the interstate away from the city I've created, and the woman who created me within it? How do I make you love and fear her as I did?

One way to reach Lala's essence is to tell you the facts: as a young child, she watched her mother die of tuberculosis, choking on her blood; she was taken in by three possibly mentally ill aunts who chopped off her hair, made her kneel on rice so often that her skin remained an open wound; she's tiny in stature but metaphorically massive, capable of flooding the kitchen with tears of anger that I didn't love her enough.

See, that's the problem with Lala and facts. I intend to stick with objective truth, and metaphors flop in and flood rooms. The truth of how I understood her bobs and slips around facts and bloats them unrecognizably.

To learn more about the semantics of translation, I went as far from Lala-land as possible: to philosophy. In his 1800 essay "On Language and Words," Arthur Schopenhauer proposes a specific marker for the mastery of a language: when the speaker is capable of translating not words but *oneself* into the other language. This issue of retaining one's character across languages remains troubling because in my distance from Spanish, I'm not sure I can accurately define who I was when I lived fully in that language. I recall my young, primarily Spanish-speaking self as devoid of personality, as completely dependent on Lala's love, as a vessel for which the only thing more powerful than the will to please was the silently brewing mutiny over my leader and her language.

When I think of who I am in Spanish as an adult, when I've spoken it with Lala, I wonder if I'm still more who she would like me to be—the loud, brash, fearless woman she once was—than I actually am. In Spanish, I search more vigilantly for the humor, the absurdity, the magic of living; I find colors and sounds bolder, more daunting; I hear in every sentence a song. It's an exhausting way to live, which may be why I don't do it (or speak it) often. To be an always-on vaudevillian in one's second, increasingly unfamiliar language is no small task.

With that in mind, allow me to translate a joke from Spanish.

Several years ago, I visited Cuba to prepare for a writing exchange the next summer between my students at the University of Alabama and Cuban students at the University of San Geronimo in Havana. As part of our "research," a colleague and I visited the Tropicana Club, famous for its lush, tropical gardens, stunning outdoor light shows, and nearly nude dancers.

We arrived early, and as I was served my first drink, an icy Cristal cerveza, an enormous bird whooshed right above me and shat all over the left side of my shoulder, my dress, my head. The mortified servers hastily brought napkins and served me a complimentary bottle of Havana Club Rum. Everyone apologized profusely: *discúlpeme*, *perdóname*. But one waiter knew exactly what to say as he dabbed my shoulder with a moist napkin: *mi niña, mejor un pájaro que un caballo*.

Better a bird than a horse.

That perfect one-liner made me forget all about the bird shit. But since then I've wondered the effect of someone saying that to me in English, after I'd been shat on by a bird of Los Estados. The joke wouldn't hold the same whimsical weight. It wouldn't be as fun. Magical realism isn't just a Latin American writing genre: it's a way of seeing the world. For a second at the Tropicana Club, I thought, yeah, I really do need to watch for those flying horses.

Two Schopenhauer connections arise from this story. For one, he contends that another touchstone for deep assimilation into any language is the ability to use its colloquialisms and humor. That tracks, because up until Lala's final days, I could still make her laugh. He also asserts we *think* differently in each new language learned, that we construct new ways of seeing that don't exist in our original language, where there may be lacking a conceptual equivalent. A further inference might be made, which is that we *feel* differently in every language too. A bird will more readily shit on me when I'm speaking and thinking in Spanish, in the language where I'll more readily laugh at it. As ludicrous as it sounds when I'm translating it now, it made sense for me to momentarily fear flying horses in Spanish.

Translating our words from Spanish to English isn't my greatest difficulty in writing about my past with Lala. It's translating her actions. What if I told you of one of the specific ways in which Lala loved: how she kissed me as a child, kissed every place, every powdered part? And that she kissed there well into the years I have memory, kissed there even when I could name those private parts, could tell her the kissing embarrassed me, struggled to find the right word that wasn't "embarrassed," something beyond *vergüenza*? How can I translate her intentions, which I'll never fully know, and yet despite all of Lala's failings, I've only ever read as absolute love? And how can I translate these even more shameful feelings: that as an adult I learned that Lala kissed Alexa, too, and how jealous this made me, since I thought Lala had loved only *me* that much, to kiss without stopping? Add to all these questions a newer revelation that casts Lala's kisses into an even more disturbing relief: that Lala *did not* kiss my other sister Aimee this way because, according to Lala, Aimee was our mother's great love, so Alexa must be Lala's. (I, having belonged to Lala all those years before Alexa's birth, now belonged to no one.) How to translate Lala's role in all this, and mine?

One way to translate it, in conceivably the way you're thinking of it now, is: *Girlfriend, this is some sick shit.* That's the way it translated years ago in my writing workshops. One peer compared Lala's love to the destructive, perverse one found in Kathryn Harrison's *The Kiss*, a memoir in which the narrator recounts her love affair with her biological father. What happened to me was abuse, I was informed, and was advised by some not to write about it. Or at least fictionalize the story, don't be *you*, Jesus, do something to make us more comfortable! Was it through these kisses, they asked, that I wanted to be known as a writer? Now, long out of the workshop, and without you here, reader, to tell me if this is how you interpret these events, I still ask myself if I can be trusted to know what I felt across my two languages and cultures.

Recently I sought my sisters' help for what I hoped would be an updated, revised translation. I visited them in Houston, where they both moved about a decade ago, and we waited until our collective nine children fell asleep to do two of my all-time favorite things: get drunk and talk shit about the past. We got our shit-talking feet wet by appraising Mom's shitty taste in men, deciding which of us has the worst father (the correct answer depends on the year in question), and then, we transitioned to Lala. In hindsight I see that when we discuss her, my sisters and I turn into little Lalas ourselves, arms akimbo or in the air, vociferous in our pronouncements about what she did right and (mostly) what she did wrong.

"The shit was abuse. It was fucked up!" says Alexa. She rarely drinks, but here she downs the rest of her red wine from her plastic flute like a pro. Like me.

I don't protest but try to reason. There are explanations for Lala's actions, if not excuses. What about witnessing her mother's death in the TB camp, the abusive aunts who repeatedly declared her unlovable, the abandonment by her father, the betrayal by her husbands, the men, the men, the men . . . ?

Both agree that parts of her life were sad, that hurt people hurt people, but as Alexa says, "She nursed us, Brooke. Our grandmother. Fed us. Her titties."

Oh, yeah. That.

Without coming off as too much a Lala-apologist, my winesplanation for this was, maybe it was culturally condoned? (I'd done no research to corroborate.) If her actions were well intended, how harmful could they have been? (Yes, this sounds like victim-speak.)

The best interpretation I can come up with is the Richard Rodriguez line from *Hunger of Memory*: "Any translation would distort the deepest meaning of her message: It had been directed only to me. This message of intimacy could never be translated." While these sentiments don't account for how Alexa interprets Lala's peculiar brands of love—and for the record, our divergent translations can simultaneously be correct—for my part, I remember Lala kissing over and under the underwear, playful, exuberant pecks, another way of saying *te quiero* bigger than the universe. What's always felt worse to me, anyway, was Lala's withholding. Her deliberate disinterest, all those easy glances away: they were brutal. I ask Aimee how she felt always being outside of Lala's crazy-strong love bubble that only ever managed to fit in one person at a time.

"Better y'all than me," she says, clinking her glass to Alexa's.

》) (《

Lala and I broke up several times through my early adulthood, once it seemed my defection to English was permanent. Our last breakup happened in my early graduate school days ("Why more college? You already know how to write!"), but we reunited after I graduated. It was a classic telenovela plotline. Tragedy in the form of natural disaster—Hurricane Katrina—brought us back together in Baton Rouge, where she lived with me for a month, feeding my dog, King, slivers of Valium and more than half of every meal I served her. She looked at me like a wide-eyed child whenever I caught her. *Yo no fui*, she'd say, quickly pulling her hand back. *It wasn't me.* I couldn't be mad at her for long because every word and action was storytelling gold. "I thought you were maybe exaggerating when you told stories about her," said my not-yet-husband. "But she's . . . out there." (He used those words, "out there." My husband is midwestern.) According to Lala, but not reality, Brock was the spitting image of a young Bill Clinton. From that proclamation forward, Lala wouldn't stop flirting with him, rolling her eyes toward heaven in ecstasy every time he spoke. But it was her lewd comments that forced me back into the world of lying in translation. In front of him, sometimes over chicken and rice, she'd declare how lucky I was to go to bed with him, asked me to describe how orgasms felt, where they resided in the body, and she'd never had one, *puedes creer?*

Perhaps this was the time when my affinity for getting drunk and talking shit about the past took full form. To counter the heartbreaking reports of our beloved city and its people drowning—physically, psychologically, even weeks after the storm—we drank and slid into old stories. Lala even joined us in the drinking once, accepting a shot of Jack. She winced, made *muecas* to lip-smack the sharp taste from her mouth, and said, "Brookecita, do you remember how I used to kiss your *chepita?*" Now I winced. "That used to annoy your abuelo so much. He would say, 'Gladys, *por favor*, she's getting too big for all that, she's going to get used to it.'"

Long pause. Batting her eyelashes. Toward me, to Brock, and back to me again. "So . . . did you get used to it?" *Te acostumbraste?*

And, I don't know, blame it on the alcohol, but with that line—*te acostumbraste*—I busted with laughter. My mother and Lala were already giggling when I translated the joke to Brock, word-for-word, as he chuckled nervously along with us. Lala felt no shame about our stories. She wanted to share them, wanted them translated, and in my desire to write them someday, I guess I was figuring out that's what I wanted too. It's the first time I can remember not having the knee-jerk impulse to lie in translation.

At the end of the month, when my mother drove Lala back to Nola on the I-10 eastbound, I saw a part of myself, my story, leaving me for what felt like the last time—at least the last time we would live together. I thought I'd flood my own house with tears.

Soon after we all recovered from the storm, Lala called me a writer for the first time. *Escritora.* It sounded syllabically a little too close to *Enriquita*, Lala's "dummy" nickname for me when she was in one of her moods. But what matters is the context in which she called me *una escritora*—she'd decided she wanted me to tell her story. *Needed* me to; this was a demand. I was elated to get her permission, though, ever her granddaughter, I was going to tell it anyway. Still, the problem remained: What story did she mean, which version? For any given incident, she held several accounts that suited her at different times. We never stole, and remember how fun stealing was? Americans chirped their detestable language, but she had no problem with English. In her entire life she'd never been loved enough, while she was also the luckiest, most beloved woman in the world.

In that same phone conversation, she said something I'd never heard before: "You're so eloquent in Spanish. I can't imagine how beautifully you're able to express yourself in English." I think I responded with the same self-deprecation I always do, like my eloquence in any language was news to me. But it later struck me that this was her first recognition that there are two Brookes, one for each language, one she had no easy access to, and she loved them both. I may not be her *cielito* anymore, but I'm her *escritora*. She'd given me a laurel I'd earned instead of just a pet name, a *cariño* meant for anybody. It was a hard-won gift, one she didn't have to steal, one I didn't have to lie for—this gift was the opposite because it required the truth. It was the best gift she'd ever given me.

It turned out we had lots of time left together after our Baton Rouge reunion, almost twelve years. During one visit in my midthirties, when Lala's dementia gripped more firmly in each successive visit, I discovered something new about the language we'd built together. When speaking, we were capable of great shallowness or great depth—no in between. For me, there's no middle ground when speaking with someone you love in a language tentative from years of disuse. We'd speak the lightest of pleasantries, *que lindo este día*, or the darkest horrors from the past, *cuando tu abuelito se murió, yo también quería morirme.* I grew tired of being either bored or devastated in her company, so I tried a new tack: I recited a poem for her. I'd enrolled in a beginning acting class at my university, and one classroom performance required the recitation of a poem. I chose Lorca's "Romance Sonámbulo" because the woman dreaming on her balcony under the gypsy moon always reminded me of Lala. I'll never know if it was true or not, but Lala had told me stories of one would-be suitor after another and their *serenadas* under her window. I added my own details to her memories, Lala on a balcony, wishing the man were someone different, Lala emerging from a turret, fearful that the climb down might be fatal, so she'd sleep to dream of her love instead of actually touching him. She'd engendered this poetry in me, so during this visit, I wanted to return it to her. I'd be the final Cyrano de Bergerac of her life, saying in someone else's words what I was incapable of expressing. "Verde viento. Verdes ramas. / El barco sobre la mar / y el caballo en la montaña." I was so proud to have memorized the first two stanzas in Spanish, twenty-four lines of inexplicable beauty, and to deliver it to her. Lala listened to the poem with her eyes closed, then opened them to the popcorn ceiling, patiently waiting for my conclusion of "soñando en la mar amarga." When I finished, she said, *ay que bello esas palabras, pero mija, no las entiento.* Beautiful, but she failed to understand. The story of our lives.

Lala died two weeks after the inauguration of the forty-fifth president of the United States, which felt to me like another kind of death. At the memorial service hosted at my mother's house, the nursing home minister who came to lead it said that the last time he saw Lala was the morning of the inauguration, where she saluted the television screen and said, with feeling—*con emoción*—how proud she was to be an American.

What? Who?

At first I thought maybe this cinctured charlatan had his own politics-via-religion agenda. Or maybe Lala had been lying to *him* in translation, or the minister had misunderstood. With Lala, who knows? A part of her may have admired the new president's flair for the dramatic, for his willingness to bend with whatever political wind might ruffle his hair-feathers. I want to believe she abhorred him as I did—that, as I tried explaining to her during my too-infrequent nursing home visits, he represented an existential crisis in American democracy. But did she even claim this country, this democracy, as hers? Another question I'll never get answered. I do know I've lived with a form of autocracy before, in the Kingdom of Lala. And it was stifling. I had no say, no vote, no voice. But I felt protected and loved, and I loved it. There is no exit ramp from this place, no change of scenery. Head east, or west, wherever the road might take you, but there is no leaving Lala for good. I'll both live in her kingdom, and miss it, always.

Now one more of Lala's stories (or is it a riddle, or a joke, or a puzzle?) that resists translation. It's another refrain of my childhood: *el cuento del gallo pelón*. The story of the bald rooster. Here's how the story went:

Lala: Do you want me to tell you the story about the bald rooster?
Me: Yes!
Lala: I didn't say anything about *yes*. I asked you if you wanted to hear the story of the bald rooster.
Me: Please, tell me!
Lala: I don't understand what you mean by *please*. I'm asking if you want to hear the story of the bald rooster.

Me: I want to hear the story! You're getting on my nerves!

Lala: Now you talk about nerves when I'm trying to tell you my story of the bald rooster.

On and on this nonstory would nightmarishly go. Through this story, neither teller nor listener ever leave the question, so the story is never finished. The act of telling (or not telling) the story is, in fact, the story. It requires the devotion of a child to continuously ask for more when resolution is out of reach. It requires a lover of language to begin the circuitous dialogue in the first place.

El cuento del gallo pelón, as is turns out, is an appropriate metaphor for all my Lala stories. I've been writing her now, with permission and without, for most of my life. Lala. Her story. What are you writing? friends ask. This story. The one I just told you about. And on and on the dialogue goes with no resolution, no end of Lala, or versions of her, in sight.

I knew Lala better than anyone; I didn't know her at all. This is my best attempt at translation.

PART II

≫⟩ ≫⟩ ≫⟩ ≫⟩ ≫⟩ ⟨≪ ⟨≪ ⟨≪ ⟨≪ ⟨≪

TWO TRUTHS
AND A LIE

ESSAYIST OR
MEMOIRIST?

≫⟩ ≫⟩ ≫⟩ ≫⟩ ≫⟩ ⟨≪ ⟨≪ ⟨≪ ⟨≪ ⟨≪

(1) I'm an essayist. This, according to essayist Vivian Gornick, means the writer uses a persona—the speaker/character she creates, who both is and is not the writer—to explore a subject other than herself. The problem, as Virginia Woolf describes it in "The Modern Essay," is how impossible it is for an essayist "never to be yourself, and yet always." That kind of paradox can be head spinning until we remember: humans contain multitudes. Any essay contains only one thin slice of a many-faceted self. But that has never been the impossible part for me. For much too long I believed that to be an essayist one required absolute expertise on one's subject (which is at least in part, oneself). I assumed understanding would come tomorrow, then tomorrow, then tomorrow. But it never came. Gornick disabused me of this notion with her line from *The Situation and the Story*, "[Essayists] may not know themselves—that is, have no more self-knowledge than the rest of us—but . . . they know who they are *at the moment of writing*." So, I merely had to have my shit figured out *on the page*, in this one thin slice, not in real life. Ooooooh. (*Enriquita*.)

(2) I'm a memoirist. The ideal memoirist, according to ideal memoirist Patricia Hampl, wishes to tell her mind, not her story. In a recent issue of *Creative Nonfiction* magazine, Hampl admits to preferring memoirists who think like essayists, writers who seek to answer more than just the quandary of how they came to be. What I want to know is the breadth of "just" in this context. As essayists, or memoirists,

what else are we truly after? Are we solving the climate crisis, global health systems, or the deep knot of racism in America? I often ruminate over these issues, but only as they apply to shit that happened to me. How else could I honestly render them? The truth is, the act of sitting down to write *anything* requires a tremendous amount of self-obsession, the relinquishment of so much living ("no time to love you now, kids, Mommy needs two uninterrupted hours of staring at her computer"). So the sooner we stop apologizing for it, the better. (I'm still sorry.)

(3) I resist categorization.

PUSH

Before you crowned and I keened for the me I'd been but could never be again and you swirled out of me like a fish, yet so unlike a fish, a voice over the hospital intercom announced *Code Silver, Code Silver*, a message we later learned meant: shooter on the hospital premises, which makes sense, since you've been born in the time of the gun, and despite hating it both as object and symbol, at that moment I considered one, since Tina, this Nurse Tina, had promised so little pushing because of all the third-trimester Pilates, and when she told me to do it, to push, I said *I am*, and when she said breathe, I said *this is how I do it*, though I couldn't be certain this was the right way, like I can never remember when I should breathe in or out for the yogic cat and cow—meanwhile the monitors go beep and outside the cars go beep and further away the cows go moo and back here the first crack of sun breaks through curtains of deep purple, dappling the linoleum and the nurse and me and the spot you're slated to be, and some would call this God but I call it you, summoning the world— and it's been hours, or days, with you and me in our first stalemate, led by this Nurse Tina, with the same name and mien as my infuriatingly evangelical aunt, so what the fuck did she know, but she came to my mind then, with that uninspired insistence of *push*, my Aunt Tina, who in my thirteenth year when I didn't trust my mother asked me not to push her away, Aunt Tina who took me to the mall and over Orange Julius wondered aloud whether or not I'd had sex yet, or done oral, the audacity of the question confounding, who then proceeded to describe her bacchanalian young adulthood, all that head and tail she gave, with the bravura of not-an-evangelical. In the breaks from pushing, when I still have a mind, I'm thinking of me at that time, thirteen and seeking love, and puzzle over the girl you'll be then, how you may often hate me, your job to live longer and learn much more than I'll ever know. To pull away. When I was ten I asked my mother to name three adjectives to describe me. She did not say "independent" or "outgoing" or "fascinating," the three correct answers, and I didn't speak to her for weeks. I won't know the answers you seek or decipher the coded questions. Hours later, after the pushing, I understand you already don't belong to me—your nostrils, your father's, the fan they create flares west, out the door. But in the before, my vagina growing steadily over those pushing hours to become a basketball, no, grander, the Taj Mahal, I watched you build me because Nurse Tina, the now-lovely Nurse Tina with all the right ideas, had asked if I wanted a mirror, placing it lengthwise at the foot of the bed, and I didn't know until that moment *yesyesyespleasethankyou*, *look at it*, *look at me*, I tell your father, who dully pumps my hand, who won't look, who is scared to, and I promised you then that I'll always look, even when it hurts, even if this is a lie, and when you finally decimate my Taj Mahal with your head, as you unfurl from me and I see what I'd known all along but could pretend wasn't true while you were inside: we are not one but two. Your role, in this time of pushing, was to leave. Sooner than I can know, your mouth will say it: *leave me alone. I don't need your help. IIIIyouyouyouyouIyouIyouI*—our names, our pejoratives, our encomiums. And now your eyes dart for discovery, for whatever we may be. I'm afraid I can't tell you what it is, that I know nothing—I'm consigned to watch helplessly during all of the breaths of your life, I realize, while they weigh you and mark you officially into the record of the world. And at last I'm born anew, too, an evangelical washed in your waters, when I first pull you into my arms.

ADDENDUM TO "McCLEANING WITH THE DUSTBUSTER"

We had babies. We bought the fucking Dustbuster.

KINGDOM OF BABES

My first was Smurfette. I found her lying in the middle of the polished floor of the TG&Y five-and-dime off Michoud Boulevard in New Orleans East, where I'd begged Lala to take me to buy my very first Smurf doll. Well, "doll" isn't the right word. When I was five, I called all my two-inch-tall plastic toys "babes," same as my five-year-old daughter calls them now. She's collected babes in the hundreds, as I once did, but as far as I know, my daughter hasn't stolen any of them.

Lala grabbed Smurfette from my hand. "*No tiene precio,*" she said, citing its absent price tag. "*Eso quiere decir que nos dan gratis.*" I didn't understand, even as she went on to explain, how something could be free if stores were inherently transactional. You gave money to get something back that you want or need. Even kids knew that.

"*¡Cállate!*" she shushed me. She set her purse down and instructed me to play with the babe directly over it and to drop her in, "*accidentalmente.*" Instead I threw Smurfette aimlessly onto the floor, sprinted down the toiletry aisle, and whisper-yelled in Spanish, "Did I do it right?" Lala quickly fixed my mistake and power walked us toward freedom there beyond the store's glass doors. She said, more to herself than me, "*Ay Dios mío, tengo que hacer todo.*" A minute later, out in the concrete heat, Lala dug through her purse to extract my prize. I held my babe close, proud of what felt not like a crime but an accomplishment. "Next time," I said, "let's take Gargamel."

≫⟩ ⟨≪

Over the years Lala delighted in helping me build my kingdom of babes, whether we bought or stole them. She often reminded me what a great joy it was to spoil me, since my single mother was always off working and no good at spoiling (Lala said "working" as if my mother were off clubbing all day, "*ay, ese trabajo*"). The hinge on whether or not to steal was the presence or absence of a price tag. Back then they were half the size of a postage stamp, or twice the size of a hit of LSD, depending on how you look at it. They were basically stickers. They included neither scanners nor bar codes. Lala got it into her head that if there was no price tag, we couldn't technically get in trouble. She'd scour through bins of toys to find one that was *limpio*, or where the tag was so flimsily applied that she could use her long fingernail to blithely slide it off. If we got questioned, we could say the item was already ours. We bought it here last week and *la niña* wanted to bring her toy on our shopping trip, and how dare they accuse us of anything, that's racist, *¡qué descaro!*

"What if there's cameras?" I once asked. I'd seen cameras capturing thieves on television, and even though those thieves were of the Hamburgler variety, wearing the "I'm about to rob you" uniform of black masks with eyehole cutouts, I was still worried about video evidence.

"*Ay, qué mierda.* We'll say we don't know who those people are, but they're not us." That Lala could be shown and deny the purest form of evidence against her and say, "nope, not me," showed the genius in her madness. And that despite herself, after years of ranting about sticking it to The Man and the *desgracio* of electing that *muñeco*-faced actor Reagan for a president, Lala had truly become an American.

What else has no price tags? we must've tacitly asked ourselves at some point. Grapes didn't, so we began routinely stealing them from Schwegmann's. They came in huge bins we'd bag ourselves and eat while we shopped, then we unloaded whatever we didn't finish back into the bin before checkout. Other fruit was up for grabs, though the gummy mess it left behind made me queasy. Once Lala ate a peach with a slow sublimity, wiping her mouth now and again with a pocket tissue, and left the pit behind some cans of tuna. In these gringo grocery stores, she also introduced me to ventriloquist eating, which was chewing while minimally moving your jaw. *Qué rico, verdad?* She insisted it tasted better that way.

We never stole anything of real value, like the 14K gold jewelry that had covered my body since birth: gold rings on each hand, gold stud earrings, a nameplate gold necklace that Lala and my mother slept me in, choking hazard be damned. Pedro Lopez, an Ecuadorian too, owned Lopez's, a jewelry shop off Veterans Boulevard in Metairie. Pedro's right eye was usually fixed through a jeweler's loupe, giving him a cyclopsian look, and his fusty breath filled the whole room. It was for these reasons, and not necessarily his racism, that I disliked him. "*Gracias a dios* I finally got the shop into a white neighborhood," he said on our first trip to his new location. Ironically, he and Lala talked about theft a lot, how he was armed, and how he wouldn't let *coño negros* come in here and take his merchandise. "But you said this was a white neighborhood," I thought to myself, trying to make sense of the senseless. I never understood Lala's hierarchy of racism either, which placed Ecuadorians at the very top, with Asian people several rungs lower (with the exception of *Chinos*, who were dirty); Black and white people lay underneath them, interchangeable depending on her mood; and Mexicans and Guatemalans sat at the very bottom. She talked a lot about *orgullo*, or pride in being one of us, but I had no idea what that meant. She pointed to no particular tradition or historical event because for her it was self-evident. Maybe I didn't want to probe it further because I was half-French-Italian, which translates to half-white, and for Lala, most whites were *caras de mierda*. Did this mean I was one-half "fuck face"? I didn't want to know. At Lopez's that day, Lala described to Pedro with gusto how thieves got what they deserved. They went straight to prison to get *culo*-fucked, she said, which led me to speculate whether Lala understood that we stole too. I scanned Lopez's rows of lighted gold jewelry, and inwardly picked out what I'd steal if I asked for Lala's permission nicely enough.

※⟩⟨※

Several years ago, as Lala was laid up in her Wynhoven Nursing Home bed and I lotioned her pale, skinny legs, I asked her if she remembered our thieving days, and why we did it. "*Estás loca*," she replied. "*Yo no fui.*" Lala's had a lifelong habit of denying or "forgetting" any memory that didn't fit her current narrative of propriety. It's true that in her last years, dementia might have caused her to forget, but when I brought up Smurfette, how I tried stealing her so ineptly, Lala winked at me. Though when I said, "*Mierda*, you winked!" she denied that too.

Like with so many of my Lala stories, I thought that the answer for her behavior was simple. She was *loca*. Or at least, she wanted to be thought of as crazy, because she loved the attention, because she thrived on being the woman who would do what others wouldn't. Once she exacted revenge on her unfaithful husband by shoving a hot pepper up his asshole, to give one perfectly normal example. But more than wanting to be thought of as powerful, she didn't want to look weak. There is a distinction.

Though we didn't discuss it, Lala was incredibly vulnerable in the world of American commerce. She never learned to speak or read English, even years after emigrating to the United States from Ecuador. But because my abuelo worked, Lala kept up their home and was expected to shop for all the things. When she wrote a check, a common form of payment in those days, she had to do it in English. So when it came time to pay, she kept a well-worn paper in the plastic covering of her checkbook, with the numerals one through one hundred written out in English. It occurs to me now, half a lifetime after our first steal, that Lala may not have wanted to ask a TG&Y employee for the price. Or even have me ask an employee for her. When we shopped for groceries, she added up the numbers in her head to get a close total estimate. Growing up, I was her translator, and she sometimes had fun with that. For instance, she'd suggest I tell an employee that he had a "*cara de verga*," thus forcing me to lie in translation about what she'd actually said, which was "penis face." But it was also a sign of weakness that she couldn't do the talking on her own. Perhaps this was why she could steal babes for me, or steal food for herself, and pretend it was an *accidente* if she got caught.

She loved lording the little power she had over others, and that often came in the form of using a language most others didn't. When I wasn't fretting over getting caught, I was concerned someone would understand Lala was talking loudly about them, since she did it constantly. Once, as we walked onto a Macy's elevator going down from the third floor, a woman in a pink pantsuit held the door open us. Lala waved her hand in front of her face and said, "*oy, esa mujer iso un pedo.*" She said the elevator stunk and accused the woman of having farted. "*¡Cállate!*" I begged her. And then, looking straight ahead, the woman responded. "*Senora, yo no fui. Sera que usted o su nieta pedo?*" She threw the accusation right back on both of us, guessing the culprit might be Lala, or me. After the woman exited the elevator, Lala called after her, "*Oye, buen hecho!*" Good one, lady! Lala laughed about the *pedo* incident the rest of the day, but I was mortified she got caught talking shit. I couldn't imagine how I'd react if we got caught stealing.

The reason we eventually stopped is because I forced it. Lala was so ostentatious about everything; it seemed like she'd be happy to get caught. Maybe she yearned for the chance to haughtily deny her theft, or to apologize for her mistake, *me-no-speaka-de-Engleesh*. I didn't wish to translate any of these potential scenarios. It was hard enough getting caught in the elevator in Spanish. If we got caught in English, the explaining would be left to me. Lala's ethos dictated that the most important thing was to be interesting, and as I slid closer to adolescence, I desired more than anything, at least for a time, to be calm, quiet, good. One day when Lala asked if I wanted a treat from the TG&Y, I said, "I'm too big for these kinds of toys." I shuttered my kingdom of babes, and that concluded my life of stealing with Lala.

My last was a couple of years ago: a box of 126 Pampers from Publix. It was an innocent-enough mistake. My grocery cart was overflowing, my then-toddler daughter was whining, and a portion of my two-hundred-plus-dollars spent was for a My Little Pony knockoff, one of my daughter's favorite types of babes. "I *need* it, Mom," she said, and who was I to argue. I finally found my checkbook in the fifth zipper compartment of my hateful purse. I often get dirty looks when I use my checkbook at the grocery. The cashier has to type in a bunch of stuff into the keypad. I sometimes imagine she's typing a message to The Man, "another loser customer writes a check." *And I guess I am a loser,* I want to scream at the cashier and the customers in line behind me, *since the reason I'm writing a check is because I don't get paid for three days and I've already figured out this grocery store doesn't cash checks for four days. I'm an underpaid English instructor, which means I'm always broke but can't righteously complain about being poor, so get off my back!* This is why I write out the check completely before I get in line, leaving blank the space for the total cost, exactly like Lala used to do. I can't imagine having to do this in a language I don't understand, since even in my fluency this simple transaction is stressful as hell.

Anyway, this was my mindset when I unloaded my cart that day. Added to this, the cashier didn't know what she was doing. She was the kind of cashier Lala would've loved, this Casey, as her nametag read. Lala would have said something simple and kind in English, "hi, girl," then in Spanish she would've loudly said "*mamahuevo*" (translated: a slightly less-harsh version of "cocksucker"). Casey was flustered from both scanning and bagging and, now, dealing with my check. I'd planned to directly hand her the diapers sitting on the cart's undercarriage, but then my daughter scooted toward the Redbox dispenser, so I had to wrangle her back. I held my daughter under my left arm and wrote out the rest of the check with the right, then helped Casey load the rest of the bags into the cart. The diapers were *gratis*; I got a thirty-dollar discount.

I wondered after I left Publix that day, and still do, if this was Lala's rationale for stealing. She had the money to get by, but maybe not as much as she wanted. A box of Pampers means lots fewer future babes. Maybe stealing helped her save where she could. Or she vaguely wanted to stick it to The Man, one of the many white ones who owned the stores and ran the world. Or it was her way of saying "fuck you" in two languages. Or she wanted to see what she could get away with. Or she wanted to teach me something about risk and reward and earning the things I liked. Or she just fucking did it and liked it. As I did, once upon a time.

If Lala were there to witness my *accidente* at Publix that day, who knows, she might have insisted that I return to the store to pay for it. And I would have, though I would remind her to recognize an interesting experience when she sees one, as she taught me. Once I exited the grocery and stepped into the concrete heat, I thought, "Next time, I'll stack a large pack of wet wipes down there, too." Like I tell my daughter when she makes a mistake, it's okay, accidents happen.

THE STUMP OF
THE GIVING TREE

Once upon a time, a dour-bearded Freud said that if a sadist and a masochist arrived at a party separately, by the end of the night the two would leave together. That's a secondhand reference from my screenwriting professor who wore cargo shorts to class every Tuesday night, propped his leg on a chair and, inadvertently or not, revealed he went commando.

Everyone knows Freud said there are no such things as accidents.

He also said, and this I've read myself, that aberrant sexual behavior begins in childhood. In my teenage years, I thought "aberrance" in children equated to my three-year-old sister fondling her clitoris in the bathtub and saying, "this feels great!" But now that I've experienced raising my three-year-old daughter who did the same, and who unlike my sister, is aberrant in nothing, I recognize this precocious massaging for what it is: basic self-care.

Years ago, as I entered college, I sought a new form of self-care when my depression loomed so large, I couldn't even turn to the books where I'd always found a home. I was down about one of those first-love breakups from which, in some ways, we never recover. My best friend's mother advised I continue being myself, and that would be survival enough (I knew I'd gone to the wrong person). Furthermore, she insisted, the reason why this relationship ended was because I was a *giver*. She was adamant about how definitively I fit into this category. I was a giver and he was a taker, so it could never work. Part of me wanted to protest: "You're wrong, we were both givers. I gave him head, he gave me HPV."

All of this context matters for how I've come to read the perennial classic *The Giving Tree* all these years later with my daughter. It's a book I want to hide, donate, "lose"; because she's a kid, she'll get over it, she has a thousand other books. But her love for it isn't why we keep reading *The Giving Tree*. Like a masochist who misses that first-breakup pain, something in me can't give it up. But the more I read it to my daughter, night after night, the more I worry I'm hurting her.

As an undergraduate, I discovered Roland Barthes's seminal essay "Death of the Author," which like most literary theories, I only superficially understood. It argued that an author's identity and biography is irrelevant to what appears in the text. Decades after discovering the theory, I'm still trying to disabuse my literature students (and myself) of the idea that authors' lives matter all that much in our attempts to understand or enjoy their work.

This knowledge doesn't stop me from asking every time I crack open *The Giving Tree*'s green spine: Is Shel Silverstein an actual piece of shit? Even the aberrant know you can't judge a book by its cover, but what about its *back cover*? Why does this dude's humongous face grace all of his books? It's either a close-up of his giant head or a medium-range shot while he sits on some exotic wicker chair, shoeless, his Wooly-Willy-esque magnetic beard artfully maintained, lips parted just so, on the cusp of imparting brilliance.

To be fair, the author's back-cover photo is a mainstay in publishing, if not such an unusually large one. Is his annoying photo the reason I attack his biography? Years ago, as I was barely finishing graduate school, having been ill prepared in my first twenty-four years of life to write the scintillating memoir I half-concocted for my thesis, a friend said, "You must finish your book soon. Write . . . anything, it doesn't matter. You won't have that pretty, young face forever." I will never know if her words were cynical or wise, because that book remains unwritten, and my rill-marked face, while not exactly old, is unlikely to be the reason why my first book sells or not.

Maybe I'm bitter that aesthetics never mattered for Silverstein's face. I won't boo-hoo about how much being a woman sucks, with unfair beauty standards and practices separating genders. But I will point out that Silverstein, esteemed children's books author, never married, and according to his own accounting, slept with hundreds, maybe thousands, of women. He frequented the Playboy Mansion. To paraphrase Barthes, who cares?

The answer is, despite theoretically knowing better, I do. J. K. Rowling was lambasted for saying shitty things about trans people, and her opinions had nothing to do with Hogwarts. Apologies to Barthes, but authorial mystique remains captivating; it mattered to us that J. K. was desperate and nearly homeless while constructing Harry. She sold us both her extraordinary fictions and the nonfiction of her life. And for all of my railing against Silverstein's peccadilloes, I warmed to him when I learned he lost one of his children, eleven-year-old Shoshanna, to a cerebral aneurysm. Does this cast his work in a new light? Shoshanna died years after *The Giving Tree* was published, and I sense what's so seemingly beautiful about the book, renowned as a treatise on unconditional love, and which I resent, is that he got to experience the glory of parenthood, the joy and the wonderment, without putting in the hard labor. Without the minutia of living with children. Without, in other words, sacrificing any of his limbs.

For those who've forgotten, here's a rundown of *The Giving Tree*. A young boy falls in love with a female tree and cuddles with her tirelessly until, alas, he grows tired of her. He reemerges at various points in the plot to hack away at her for capitalistic purposes: apples, leaves, branches, trunk, all of which he sells off or builds up to make himself happy. Meanwhile, the female tree is just so grateful to be useful to the boy she loves dearly, till all that's left of her is stump. Finally, as the boy cradles death's door, he returns for a place to sit and presumably die on, and there's the tree stump, straightening herself to be of final service. The tree is awash in joy because the boy deigned to remember to die on top of her. The end.

Awwww, say millions of readers, who have wept at the ostensible message of generosity and beauty.

Would I feel more warmly toward the book if the tree were a *he*?

I don't know. I doubt it would've gotten published that way because this parable required the tree to be maternal, to give whatever the cost, to be the quintessential happy martyr.

My reaction may be wrong because I'm foregrounding the male/female relationship here, rather than the parent/child dynamic—more specifically mother and child. To commemorate Toni Morrison's death in 2019, I reread *Sula* for the first time in years and stopped cold during this passage about the finite love between mothers and children. Here the mother, Nel, was recently abandoned by her husband who left her for her best friend, Sula. Initially, Nel takes comfort in her children's love: at least this is a love, Nel tells herself, that will last. But wait, warns the narrator:

> [The children] were all she would ever know of love. But it was a love that, like a pan of syrup kept too long on the stove, had cooked out, leaving only its odor and a hard, sweet sludge, impossible to scrape off. For the mouths of her children quickly forgot the taste of her nipples, and years ago they had begun to look past her face to the nearest stretch of sky.

I was so stunned by that passage, I took a picture of it with my phone and put the book down for a day, staring at the photo-less back cover. I needed to think hard about my life.

Why does my daughter love *The Giving Tree*? Why does she spend so many nights asking for it again and again? During one of our reads, I ask her.

"It's beautiful," says Mina, drawing out the *ooo* in her mouth. She's staring at the book's title page, the tree bent over and beckoning the boy with her lithe limb-arms.

"That's true," I say. "But you know that real beauty comes from our insides. Like strength. It's not about big muscles but big hearts. Which is also a muscle, but you get it."

"No, I don't. The heart is a muscle?"

"Yes." I love when I can answer something definitively as a parent.

"What does inside beauty look like?"

Dammit. "It's hard to describe. You can't see kindness or goodness or compassion or caring, but those things are inside you, and those things are beautiful parts of you. Loving others as you love yourself."

Mina is kindness incarnate; if girls on the playground refuse to include her in their play, her enormous heart muscle tearing, she commends them for having the right idea. A few months ago we drove to the park, during Covid times, and I shivered at the sight of several girls on the swing set, clearly intimate, with their two mothers lounging under a gazebo. An already-formed friend group, my worst nightmare. Mina was, of course, dismissed by an older girl, but a surprisingly nice little blonde shared my daughter's unicorn mania, so they made a tenuous connection. I hid my tears behind my sunglasses; I fear any rejection she might face more than my own. The lounging women's tacit exclusion by ignoring me was fine, I don't need adult conversation, just as long as my daughter is happy, and oh my God I'm the quintessential martyr giving tree.

What I mean to say in all this: I want my daughter to be harder than I am. I've so often been the Giving Tree, offering away my own body and heart till I've felt like little more than a stump, with a stump's personality. "Too long a sacrifice / can make a stone of the heart" said Yeats in "Easter, 1916," of Irish revolutionaries, bypassing the terrible beauty borne by mothers who fight mostly with themselves: unaware, eventually, of what and why we're sacrificing to begin with.

Mina continues her praise of *The Giving Tree*. "I love how kind she is. I love being kind."

"That's great, but not too much."

"I thought it was impossible to be too kind."

I scan her room for inspiration, for metaphor. Her pink walls, gauzy pastel curtains. She's loved being a girl, so we've surrounded her with girliness. This room's one exception is the austere wooden shelving. Five shelves, wide panels, a professor's bookshelf. It's here because it didn't fit in the living room. For now it's filled with popular and classic kids' books, from E. B. White to Madeleine D'Engle and, yes, Shel Silverstein. Eventually I'll help her fill it with whatever I want for her. I mean, what we want. I mean, what she wants.

I tell her that's mostly true, but it's a fine line to tread, and I'm too tired to explain the nuance.

"What's nuance?"

Someday I'll get all this right.

Mina's younger brother, Manny, is almost two years old and not talking yet, and I've decided not to freak out about that. He understands his desires and how to fulfill them, even without language. Throughout his infancy while nursing, his emotional dessert involved clamping down on my nipple and shaking his head back and forth lightly, a dog with a chew toy, till he unexpectedly pulled backward hard, stretching me like taffy. While this moment motherfucking hurt, I'll be damned if I didn't get enjoyment *every time* from seeing his sweet smile afterward. The Giving Tree doesn't literally smile in the book, since she has no face, but she is clearly thrilled each time the boy takes away a piece of her. I get it. I'm scared already of my children looking past my face to the nearest stretch of sky. Even though, of course, that's what they were born to do. To separate. Become.

Manny has zero interest in *The Giving Tree*. Slytherin as we've lovingly dubbed him, he's ripped apart many nonboard books, so I've purposefully left it in his room, hoping he'd make confetti out of it. But he doesn't. I've started asking myself if he knows something I don't.

In 2011, a few years out of graduate school and contemplating having children, I read Francis Ford Coppola's advice to young artists. Here's a paraphrase: *If you're a man, marry young. Your need to provide will make you hungrier to successfully launch your career.*

If you're a woman, he said, *don't get married. Or if you must, marry late. Prioritize yourself and get your work done before family consumes everything.*

I'd split the difference on this advice. I was a young writer married to another writer, three years at the time. In second-wave feminist fashion, I'd eschewed taking Brock's last name, Guthrie. Four years later, in patriarchal fashion, we began having Guthrie children. In the interim, we settled into a marriage of giving and taking, each to each, learning to be either tree or boy when we needed to be. This calibration deprioritized our writing, but we were happy. There was no "husband and wife" about us. Just a marriage, growing roots.

Since having children, I've been guilty of participating in what I swore I never would, which is noting how my kids behave according to their genders. She's sensitive; he's tough. She's cuddly; he's a loner. She delicately admires books; he rips them apart. I've tried to correct this inner monologue by outwardly reminding my daughter how strong she is, and my boy, how sweet he is. Though I do wonder if my private thoughts might engender their behaviors.

Coppola's advice was old-school and a touch paternalistic, and also, it did not help me, but I'm adopting it for my own children. As I've read *The Giving Tree* to my daughter, and considered what it might be like to read it to my son and the messages it sends to each of them, I've come away with an answer for making the book as useful as possible. I want Manny to be the tree, and Mina to be the boy. Remember, Mina: love is leaving, having adventures, discovering who you are away from the pages of the book I've written for you. Remember, Manny: love is staying, it is tenderness and humility; it is compromise.

Then again, I cannot contain my children in any essay or book I'll ever write. Mina might defy me by becoming the tree. Manny might become the boy. They will make these decisions about themselves, through a million books and media and interactions and inflections, despite my desires. No matter how I rail against gender norms or conditioning, there they'll be. And, dammit: so what if I'm the stump. It's still an existent thing. A stump literally creates the pages on which I write. A stump contains roots unseen. A stump's roots are so long, they've experienced enough sadism and masochism to leave the great cosmic party by themselves. But before the party's over for me, if either of my children asked, I wouldn't hesitate. Maybe I'd even find strength in the terrible beauty of it. For them I'd hack off my limbs, and remain limblessly happy. The end.

DON'T YOU
FORGET ABOUT ME

Outside our two-bedroom duplex on Thirtieth Street in Lakeview, one of several New Orleans neighborhoods where my mother and I made our fatherless homes, I once tried to enter through the side door and found it locked. I'd been playing under the carport with my Cabbage Patch Kid, Suzy Georgette, whose packaging promised she'd be my best friend. I hadn't yet downgraded to Garbage Pail Kids, their perverted parody, whose cynicism better befitted the Gen X ethos of hating everything, including things we loved. This neighborhood felt more humid than others, courtesy of that dirty gray water-blanket of Lake Pontchartrain pulled up tight to the neck of our city. I couldn't take a step without slipping in the sweat inside my jelly shoes. Even my Cabbage Patch looked wilted. After I knocked for, like, forever, my mother at last opened the door.

"Mom, why did you lock me out?"

"Oh, hello. Who are you?" My mother was chopping carrots at the cutting board next to the sink, focused, careful. I hated carrots. She hated cooking.

"What do you mean, Mom?"

"Little girl, you seem very sweet, but you're not my daughter." She set down her knife and leaned against the counter, pulling a Virginia Slim from her gold lamé cigarette case. That case smelled sharp, like burnt metal, but my mother always managed to smell soft, like Chloe powder.

"You should go home now." She looked directly into my eyes and exhaled. "Your real mother must be worried about you."

Then she led me out the door again and shut it; I heard the click of the lock. I sat on the carport steps and wailed, "But you *are* my mother, right! Right?" Tugging at the sweaty bangs stuck to my forehead, literally pulling my hair out to make sure I existed, I wondered what was real in the world—was this a nightmare? My supposed best friend was no help. Finally, my mother opened the door again and reassured me of the truth I'd thought I'd always known: she was my real mother, and this was my home.

"Why did you believe me?" she said. "Honey, I was kidding!"

Nothing to worry about here, it's only a game. Until the next time she decided to play it.

My mother's "You're Not My Daughter" game recently became a subject between me and my own four-year-old girl. I told her about it because I was afraid my inner imp would emerge as my daughter was learning new and terrifying things about the world—death, for one, but also the million global crises I've invited her into that neither of us can do much about. Maybe I'd tease her as my mom teased me, to toughen her up. I also told her about it because, frankly, I wanted her to side with me over the game's injustice, its insanity.

Like mothers immemorial, I've spent a lot of time choosing which parts of my mother I'd adopt in my parenting, and which I'd repudiate. "You're Not My Daughter" proved a special case. The game instilled self-loathing for my dupability and, obversely, self-confidence to struggle honorably through adversity; both qualities have served me well. But I don't want my daughter writing in her diary, as I did soon after my mother first played this game with me, "I. Hate. M-O-T-H-E-R," where my rebuke took up several months of 1986's daily pages. On the other hand, I don't want my daughter's personality to be so glutted with sweet, gummy love that she'll have no sense of humor. If I couldn't raise her in my hometown of New Orleans, she'd adopt its ethos. Laissez Le Bon Temps blabbedy-blah.

What I wasn't expecting was my daughter's own imp. Last spring as I drove her home from preschool, she asked what colleges were for (a question I've often asked myself). It's a place you go, I said, ideally away from your hometown, to become a better citizen, to learn how to learn, to study for the career and life you want. I graciously left out the part about descent into extraordinary debt from which she'd never climb. She wondered aloud if New York City had any colleges she could attend. We'd visited family there the year before and she loved it.

"Oh honey," I said, "there's tons! You can go to NYU, and then I can visit you in the city!"

"Actually," she mused from her car seat, "I'm not sure if I'll let you visit me." I adjusted the rearview to see her face. She gazed contemplatively out the window.

"Why not?"

"I think you should have to stay home while I'm in college and wait for *me* to visit *you*. When I feel like it."

I readjusted the rearview back to the road, blinking away tears. If I were my mother, I'd say, "See if I invite you home for Thanksgiving then, you little shit!" But I'm not. My fears were already coming true: my daughter would hate me someday or be bored by or forget about me once she'd extracted every atom of love.

"Sorry to hear that," I said, my voice wavering. "Let's talk about something else."

"Mom, oh my gosh, I'm kidding!" She giggled and kicked the back of my seat. "You don't always have to believe me."

Though I'm old enough by now to sit comfortably with most forms of rejection, I'm not sure I'm ready to handle my daughter's version of "You're Not My Mother." I know the havoc these kinds of games can wreak. But it can't just be Mom's early teasing games that account for why I'm having more trouble communicating with her now than thirty-five years ago. No, for this I blame neither our personalities nor idiosyncrasies, but our generations.

While there's some disagreement over the precise dates of my generational cohort, most social science researchers, including the Pew Research Center and Nielsen Media Research, now typically use the birth years between 1965 and 1980 to define Generation X. I was born in October 1980, which according to this date range, makes me one of the youngest, therefore least cool, members of my generation. Unfortunately, coolness and iconoclasm are what my generation is all about. Not only am I nearly left out of this group I've always wanted to belong to (and according to many Xers, having been born in the eighties manifestly designates me a Millennial), I was the firstborn child in an immigrant family on my mother's side. My brown skin coupled with having been raised by Ecuadorian women precludes me from being white, while my caca Spanish shuts me out of being brown. My first-ever concert starred Julio Iglesias at the historic Saenger Theater; my second, at the monstrosity of the Louisiana Superdome, featured New Kids on the Block. A proud Gen Xer might laud the first for being so antimainstream that the performance wasn't even in English, and eye roll the second as integral to the downfall of American culture.

That maybe says it all about where I fall racially, generationally, and psychically. I've been disaffected from my peers for as long as I can remember, while simultaneously craving that disaffection. I learned the genius of Bob Dylan not from his unforgettable catalog, but from the transcendentally forgettable 1988 movie *The In Crowd*, which imagined a 1960s where America's hottest dancer was a skinny, backstory-less blonde. I didn't pine for Nirvana till after Kurt died, and I didn't discover Paul Westerberg and The Replacements till last month, but the quality of being left out of so many cultural aspects of Gen X while also having lived through them is, in its own way, very X. It's definitely X to have felt as a child that I belonged nowhere, with no one, except with Suzy Georgette and my subsequent collection of Garbage Pail Kids, both of which I lost and mourned stoically during one of our moves.

The paradox in defining Generation X is that the X itself refers to an unknown variable, or a desire *not* to be defined. Jeff Gordinier, author of *X Saves the World*, exudes irony even in his title. He cites the single question on the Generation X Aptitude Test: *Do you want to change the world?* If the very question makes you want to throw up in your mouth, congratulations! You're part of the most forgotten generation in demographic history. And yet according to Gordinier, that's Gen X's greatest fear, being forgotten. He emphasizes our collective *athazagoraphobia*, and how it was built into our systems. The term refers not to just being ignored between the mammoth generations surrounding us—Boomers and Millennials—but also the act of forgetting itself: forgetting who we've been and who we wanted to be. Xers famously forgot their against-the-grain ideology when they realized there was money to be made through dot coms, a movement for which I was too young to sell out. But I'd like to think I wouldn't have forgotten any ideals I'd demanded of myself, since I've always held that constant craving for self-definition and identification. Yet there's nothing more uncool, or un-X, than that. I'm not sure if it derived from my mother's early "forgetting" of me, but my whole life I've basically been asking the older kids of my generation, "Can I be part of your group?" The inevitable answer: um, *no*.

I've recently recognized that the act of forgetting, or the quality of being forgettable, is crucial to "You're Not My Daughter." Whenever I've discussed the game, the onus has been on my mother as major inciter and player. But a question I'm finally asking myself is, why the hell did I fall for it? I've considered the following possibilities for my reaction:

1. When she pretended not to be my mother, it was pure renunciation; she didn't love me anymore. So my neurotic hair pulling and tears were justified. However, this scenario also makes me a victim and my mother a villain, two overly simplistic identifiers I loathe. But with the next option . . .
2. I could play the hero. My mother had amnesia! She'd forgotten I was her daughter and I had to perform some feat to prove it to her . . . but what? Only with Baby-Sitters' Club President Kristy Thomas–like pluck would I prevail. But the true Gen X response would have included a third possibility . . .

3. Acceptance that my mother was a bored, lonely Boomer who needed to play this game more than even she knew, so I should eye roll it until she's gotten her kicks.

But I was a kid when this game began, so my original theoretical framework was *waaaaah*. Under the Thirtieth Street carport, whenever she'd banish me yet again, helpfully suggesting I go find my real mom, I learned to stop crying because that made the game last longer. For each occasion we played, I wondered if *this time* she was telling the truth. Maybe she'd taken me back in previously out of pity and had only been pretending to be my mother. Or, was it possible that *I'd* forgotten who my real mother was? The whole thing was an enormous head trip. Eventually I reminded myself, as Axl Rose assured me a few years later with his cold November rain, that nothing lasts forever. To pass the time until my mother would admit I was her daughter, I made up little games for myself and Suzy Georgette, games I could actually win.

These days my mother feels guilty about having played it, but I suspect that's because, when she's shared the story with friends and colleagues, they've found it appalling. "Jesus, Rosita," they say. "I hope you're paying for her therapy!" (She is not. But she does give me gas money every time I return to New Orleans.)

My mother tries to explain herself. "I don't know why I started it. I had no idea you'd react that way," she said during my last visit. "But when you did . . . shit, your hysterics made me laugh." Her defense included that she didn't solely abuse me; she'd tried to spread it out evenly among her younger daughters as well.

"But they rolled their eyes so hard when I pulled 'You're Not My Daughter.' They'd go, 'Whatever, Mom, you're so stupid,' and that's when the game died. No one was as fun as you." It's another humiliation that my younger sisters, born eight and ten years after me, thus firmly ensconced Millennials, are in this way much more Gen X than I am.

In this past year, we youngest Gen Xers turned forty, appropriately, in the middle of a global pandemic. Talk about being forgotten. Who, including me, could possibly give a shit about my aging milestone amid such mass, protracted devastation? Nevertheless, I persisted. But it didn't help that my daughter's birthday is the very day before mine, thus invalidating any proper celebration of my birth, I expect, for the rest of my life. After a two-week quarantine, we spent the weekend at Mom's house on the Westbank of New Orleans, where my mother set up pink unicorn decorations for my daughter, and a black-ballooned, over-the-hill theme for me.

The festivities ultimately fell apart because of a single word. My mother asked me to fill my daughter's plastic unicorn party tray with an enormous bag of Mars Mini Chocolates. Given that only family was present, and we also had two giant cakes to eat, I filled the tray halfway. My mother chastised me for this candy-filling underperformance. "Oh my gosh, you're so useless." Rather than defend myself, or address my hurt at her comment directly, I stomped around and slit my eyes whenever she spoke, which was code for, "apologize immediately." Then the obsessive ruminations began. Was I truly *useless*? It's true I can't cook well or interpret any manual's instructions or throw parties or do really anything women (humans?) are supposed to know how to do. Was the comment purely situational, or did she mean something more insidious? My mother happily overflowed the tray and, I'm guessing, forgot about our interaction before she unwrapped the first chocolate and popped it in her mouth.

Luckily, Mom's birthday present of a handle of Maker's Mark bourbon helped me sluice through my thoughts. Measured another way, a handle holds thirty-nine shots, presumably one for each year I've squandered. It came with a personalized tumbler that read, "1980 Vintage—Aged to Perfection." My mother would soon deeply regret both these gifts. Hours after unwrapping, I threw an epic fit over "useless" comparable to the "You're Not My Daughter" days. I cried, of course. I got my husband involved when I demanded he order my mother to stop being mean to me. I jabbed my finger behind me, at the past, I guess. I distributed every old hurt I could think of like party favors for everyone to take with them as a memory of the day.

The morning after, I made my walk of shame to my mother's bedroom and took back all my grievances. I blamed the pandemic; I blamed my newly diagnosed perimenopause; I blamed it on the alcohol; and most importantly, I blamed my own sensitive character, the cause of many a family dramedy. "Let's forget about it," I pleaded. And against my very nature, for a while, I did too.

But a year later, a question I'm finally asking myself is why the hell did I throw this fit? Which expressions were drunken, weary pandemic tantrum, and which did I mean? Three statements I remember making in between sobs:

1. "I was so *lonely* as a child!"
2. "I'm not sure you *loved* me!"
3. "I always felt so *unseen*!"

In sober retrospection, only one of those statements was real. When my mother "forgot" who I was those decades ago, it was like she couldn't see the authentic me: her daughter. If even that identifier was in doubt, what hope did I have of being anything else? This line of questioning makes it clear how much I required constant positive reinforcement. Shit, I still do. I'm needy. I've always wanted my mother to tell me who and what I am because I didn't have the confidence to name it for myself. I needed her to sanction my very breath. Yet she was of the generation and disposition of needing me, in turn, to figure out breathing on my own. My mother shows love in the ways that I should yearn for, X-wise, but paradoxically renounce. In motherly love and support, she's much less pink unicorn decoration and more black balloon. Like, she's never been a big hugger, or told me I'm amazing, but she'd cut a bitch for me. When I was in college, she threatened my low-key-stalking ex-boyfriend that if he didn't leave me alone, she'd tell the world he had a tiny dick. Though she couldn't have known that fact, it was perhaps by virtue of being true that her threat worked; I never heard from him again. Her love was always present, even in the days of "You're Not My Daughter." Lala informed me years afterward that my first Cabbage Patch Kid, Suzy Georgette, the one I lost and eventually forgot about, had cost way more than my single mother could afford, but I'd forcefully underlined it on my Christmas list. At the Kmart where she bought it, Mom nearly had to knock another mother's teeth out to get the last one on the shelf.

Maybe I have such a hard time belonging in any of my roles—mother, daughter, Xer—not just because of my mother's games but because I don't belong to a fully formed generation at all. In 2014, writer Sarah Stankorb, born in the same year as me, promulgated in *Good Magazine* the term "Xennial," a newly invented generational cohort that explained why Americans born in the late seventies and early eighties feel like we don't fit into our neighboring eras. Her article describes those born between 1975 and 1985 as a "micro-generation," blending the mopey dissatisfaction of Gen Xers and the cheerful confidence of Millennials. The first mutt generation in social science, it marries its surrounding groups into the ugliest portmanteau imaginable, but it pretty accurately describes my cultural personality. Being an Xennial should appeal to me, a displaced generation within a generation. Still, with the ferocity and focus of a Millennial, I insist I'm X. Like all sensible theories that contradict what I believe to be true and holy, I'm ignoring this one. In fact, I've already forgotten about it.

What I can never forget, though I've tried, is the power that the games I played as a child still hold over me as an adult. And it's not just my mother's. More than any other doctrine—the Golden Rule, the Ten Commandments, "You're Not My Daughter"—it's a game I invented for myself that has shaped my relationship to others and fed my obsession with hierarchy and self-definition. The game: any person who was born *any time* before me, on October 12, 1980, at precisely 7:31 p.m., "beats" me. If they're even a second older than me, they have the advantage. Even the worst people, like white nationalists or P.E. teachers. It's not that I believe anyone older than me is a good or moral person, or anyone younger, a bad or lesser one; it's that I've created an arbitrary yet exacting system for appraisement, and

I'm sticking to it. There's no allowance in our collective selves for genius or ordinariness or depravity. The single criterion for having the slight edge is whether or not the moment of a person's birth comes before or after mine.

Under the foolproof paradigm of "But What's Your Birthdate," Elon Musk edges me out, but I beat Mark Zuckerberg. I also beat Kim Kardashian, because I was born three days before her in 1980. Kanye West was born the same year as my husband and three before me, so they both have the damn edge. More poignantly, the game grants easy perspective on my successes and failures as a writer. For instance, if another writer at least one second older than me has great success, it's because of this arbitrary (yet significant!) extra time alive. If any writer at least one second younger than me has great success (and these numbers are growing, growing, growing . . .), well, their success simply doesn't mean as much. Because by virtue of my being born first, I understand something ephemeral about living on this Earth that they cannot yet touch. They are, let's face it, striving Millennials (or Zoomers!), while I am the elusive, unknown variable of X. Listen, I'm not proud of this notion. It's simplistic, absurd, and adds nothing to my understanding of anything. Yet I cling to it like scripture someone else wrote for me and demanded I live by. But hey, other people do that too. If this were my religion, and it kind of is, it would be callous to judge me too harshly for it.

I first played this game with myself while sitting under the Thirtieth Street carport wondering if my mother was genuinely my mother. "But What's Your Birthdate" countered well against "You're Not My Daughter" because my game had a clear winner and loser, and any victory or defeat was totally out of my control. Not only that, but it was a game I always won, even if I was younger than my rival, since no one but me ever knew we were even playing it. When a family moved in next door to us on Thirtieth, I was excited to learn they had a daughter about my age. But *how* old, precisely? This was the first question I asked Melissa. Not her age, but her birthdate. January 1981. It was my first victory, after the one over Suzy Georgette, who was "born" in 1983.

Thirty-five years since my game's inception, it's still one I play privately, constantly, during conversations with acquaintances who assume I'm having normal thoughts, or that I'm listening to them. When I first meet someone, I tactfully slip in a question about their age, often by asking when they graduated high school. If we graduated in the same year, I get nervous because I know I'm in contention, and then I must ferret out their season of birth. Because I was born in the fall, I always pray for winter. All this birthdate work takes some mental acuity, time I could have spent solving my other personal issues or even changing the world, if I were interested in that sort of thing. But paramount in my mind, always, is whether or not I have the pointless edge.

As perversely superficial as my game is, I love playing it. And I thank my mother for that. "You're Not My Daughter" needed supplanting by play of my own creation. My mother's game taught me to question my identity early on, and that my identity was malleable. *Was* I my mother's daughter? What does it mean to be such a thing? Am I X, or Xennial, and to what degree do these designations make me *me*? My mom's response to all this analysis, I'm sure, would be to tease me for trying too hard to make meaning out of everything; to this critique, I'd give her shit for not analyzing *enough*. Her newest favorite taunt deputizes her as a Burr to my Hamilton, ribbing me for presuming I'm the smartest in the room. Shows what she knows. According to "But What's Your Birthdate," a game I've never shared with her, since she was born first, *she* has the edge.

I don't intend to play any of these games with my daughter. As my mother has suggested, no matter what I do, I'll inadvertently torture my girl. My mother says, "Watch. She'll come to you in thirty years and complain, 'Why didn't you play "You're Not My Daughter" with me? That means you didn't love me enough!'" And she may be right. But I'm starting to think this wasn't uniquely a game my mother played with me. It seems representational, one that allowed us to define who we were against each other, one generation to the next. Her generational purview has been, in relation to her children: in moments, I'll intentionally forget about you to better remember myself, and I'll always leave some parts of that self locked away, and this will grant you the freedom to make something totally original out of the unknown variable that is you. Because of her "forgetting," I started writing that I hated her, then editing those diary entries later to say I loved her, and I haven't stopped writing since. Because of her "forgetting," I could never forget myself. Her games resulted in what I can only call accidental good parenting. I'm not sure there's any other kind.

What I want for my daughter, a member of a generation yet to be named, is to invent her own games and form her own theories, as deep or erroneously shallow as my own. Then we'll have competing theories to argue over, and we'll always have something to talk about, always more atoms of love to share. Plus, I can take private comfort that no matter what she says or believes or discovers, ever, she won't have the edge. I will. Because she was born after me.

EXERCISES

By a small sample may we judge of the whole piece.
—Cervantes, *Don Quixote*

ANECDOTE

That last night, we accidentally surprised him. Having changed our minds about staying over at my mom's after a French Quarter poetry reading, we drove back home to Baton Rouge where Dad was living with us. Perhaps a minor fight between Brock and I earlier that night about my father—that he had no plans to find work or leave our house, ever—precipitated our change of plans. In the beginning, Hurricane Katrina's devastation was universal and personal: but also an opportunity for my father and me to rebuild our fraught relationship. That was six months ago; this, now, was a very different time.

After we closed the car doors gently, we didn't jingle the keys as we'd gotten used to doing, warning him of our arrival. Noiselessly, we opened the front door and entered the living room, and in a moment, Dad had whirled up from the sofa and turned toward us, hand covering himself, zipping up his pants. Bodies fucked loudly, wildly, on the screen. Brock, Dad, me frozen in that instant in the living room.

We'd ignored it the other times, ignored lots. But now Brock threw up his arms and said, "What are you doing, dude? You're standing in your daughter's house with your penis in your hand!"

As they exchanged more words, I performed the emotional equivalent of stopping my fingers in my ears. I said nothing. In the morning my father was gone and left no sign of where he went. Though back in touch and reconnected years later, Dad and I have never spoken of this time.

BRITISH GOTHIC

From the halcyon night, Mr. Guthrie and I stepped into the living room, dark but for the colors on the television screen, rays emitting a bluishness, reflecting the sadness of Mr. Champagne, a man who no longer believed in love, who in fact was once quoted as saying, "The idea of my falling in love again, ever, is hilarious," and I may have remembered this in that instant—love, no longer an option, why might he not explore the variegated ways in which one finds erotic pleasure, if not in warm, tender flesh, then in pixelated two dimensions, though alas, the literal den of iniquity was *my* den, thus, the seat of impropriety. Within our young couple's hearts: that growing love for each other, so passionate and full without the need for pixilation, and by extension, our uncertainty, desperation to proceed together into the future on our own. So Mr. Champagne listened to Mr. Guthrie's mournful words; hours later, perchance within the witching hour, he fled the house, never to return.

TANKA

Left door unlocked, now
    we can't get in. Dad's there, dick
in hand, porn on, then
    shouting—who doesn't belong,
who does. Spring night. Years await.

BLURB

In her latest essay, the author of several other works about her father makes meaning of the six-month period he lived with her after Hurricane Katrina ravaged the city of their births and left him, not for the first or last time, homeless. The work will focus particularly on their last night living together in the author's home—or, is that night more of an afterthought in the essay? Modeled after Raymond Queneau's seminal *Exercises in Style*, in which Queneau tells the same pedestrian anecdote about a man on a bus through dozens of forms in order to show the beauty of seeing the situation differently, this iteration of *Exercises* seeks to illuminate the prismatic nature of not just situation but story when told in multitude. And here lies what separates the two works: this author's anecdote is more personal than Queneau's, thus more changeable. In order to understand it, we must hear it told in many different voices, or not at all. Or at least, this is her understanding of Queneau's work during the period in question, when reading and rereading the French author's simple assemblage of exercises was easier than parsing out her big one: *Who is father, and who am I?* Her resultant attempts to answer the unanswerable many times over becomes an irreverent, Proustian unfolding of the Japanese paper flower in muddy water, a thin slice of their lives in all its mildewed multiplicity.

APOSTROPHE

O oft-dropped Dell Inspiron 1520, be the humble receptacle of this truthful tale, which like most experiences, lives in the past, present, and future, & let finger flicks & clops of hand heels unfurl words onto that virtual white screen in the Times New Roman stamp of familiarity. O, be the venue for thy lover, future husband, baseball-hatted and beleaguered, and thy father, hunched over, member in hand, one sock pulled high, the other's errant elasticity amassed around his ankles the night in question, lo those many years ago. O though the details of his stay be too numerous to recount—thy father's slumped shoulders bearing some infinite anguish, the meals he prepared with unwashed-handed abandon (salty ham hocks, spaghetti topped with hard boiled eggs—foods served by a foreigner, to be politely smiled through), the gallons of liquor purchased in those months to shepherd all three of you across the River Lethe to forget—let now the sins of inebriation wash away so that the truth of this past & selves live on the page, arisen from the murky waters of memory!

DRUNK

Dick in his hand y'all, I'm not kidding. Muthafucka stood up quick and was all like, *ooh, no, what y'all doing home so early, y'all want something to eat, here, let me go fix some ham hocks for ya, let me tuck myself away right quick. Oh, y'all ain't hungry, well, I think I'll go to bed . . .*

And Brock's like, hold on, we're not having any more of this dick-in-hand shit, you've got a daughter, she loves you, you better look like getting your shit straight and get a job, FEMA money doesn't last forever, what are you doing, dude . . .

And I was like, damn, I'm gonna marry that mutherfucka.

PRECISION

The address: 1707 Cloverdale Dr., Baton Rouge, LA 70808. The room: roughly six hundred square feet, the television a thirty-inch Panasonic from Walmart, the largest purchase made with the father's $15,000 FEMA windfall from the flood loss of his mother's Gentilly Woods home, the bodies on the television clenched on a king-sized bed taking up about half of those television inches. Inside the DVD player, a pornography disk starring Jada Fire, rented from Major Video two blocks down at 3655 Perkins Road. The older man standing in front of the television in the living room weighing 159 pounds, his daughter 141, the boyfriend 182. The couch: full length, cream colored, six feet long. On the coffee table, framing the scene, sits a 1.75 liter handle of Jack Daniel's Old No. 7 Whiskey, bought (presumably) hours before from Martin's Wine Cellar on 7248 Perkins Road for $19.97. Approximately 350 milliliters of Jack consumed prior to our entrance, though that's a difficult thing to measure by looking.

TELENOVELA

Hijo de la granputa madre! Dígame porque vives haci, porque no buscas empleo, porque son tus días tan secas, sin vida? Por favor, senior, no puedes seguir viviendo haci en esta casa, por diosito santo!

Q: Did you purposefully sneak up on your father that night?

A: No!

Q: Then why didn't you jingle the keys so he'd hear you, as you'd done before?

A: I don't know . . . I think we were getting tired of having to be thoughtful of *his* needs in *our* house.

Q: Why didn't you speak during the incident?

A: I was scared of being angry. I'd never lived with my father. I was scared of his leaving after having stayed all that time. But I was also scared of his staying. Scared of choosing my boyfriend and our future over me and my dad's.

Q: Haven't you admitted to being relieved after you woke up to find him gone?

A: Haven't *you* ever heard of cognitive dissonance? Feeling two opposing ideas at once?

Q: Don't be a smartass. Couldn't you have treated him better?

A: Yes. When I reached out to take care of my father, something pulled me away. It wasn't the porn, though it was easy to point a finger there. I wanted to be taken care of, be vulnerable, do the hiding from him, rather than having to find him. I was helping him, so I couldn't call out for help, and I resented him for it.

Q: So why are you telling this story now?

A: I've always wanted to tell it, but didn't know how. I felt we shared a temporary joint custody of this story, me and my dad, and telling it on my own would mean a nasty divorce. I didn't want that. I still don't. I just want to know him better. More than that, I want him to know *me*. Telling the story is my oblique means of feeling closer to him.

Q: Are you certain you want to know and share his stories in order to become closer as a father and daughter, or, as a writer, are you trying to cannibalize him by creating this unique, interesting character?

A: Fuck.

Exercises

Q: Do you in fact love your father?

A: What kind of thing is that to say?

Q: I'm the one asking the questions here.

ASIDES

The door was unlocked (*we weren't supposed to be back this soon*) and porn was on the TV, and Dad was half-dressed and alone, and later, I realized, lonely (*the one woman I've ever known him to date was a criminal named Deanna, who was serving time for drug trafficking—and Dad told me once how when she was ten years old she learned how to steal from an ATM using bubble gum and yo-yo string, and I'd never seen him look so proud, and that hurt*). Brock yelled at my father—he'd been lounging around too long, it was time to go (*Brock and I were married two years later—he was my hero that night for speaking up when I wasn't able, yet his words released my father into the world again without me, and that hurt too*). Dad didn't say much for himself, and I didn't say anything (*we didn't speak in those intervening years, either, and right before my wedding, my father—uncharacteristically, I thought—called with an offer to walk me down the aisle*). I slowly backed out of the room to cry in bed (*I told my father I'd be walking down the aisle alone, that it was symbolic of my independence . . . or something*). My father was gone the next morning (*I regret that now, my silence that night before he left, and walking down the aisle alone years later. I could've used his arm*).

THIRD-PERSON PAST

Before that spring night with the locked door and porn and penis-in-hand, before he reappeared in her life and left again, she missed him. Her father and mother separated before she was two years old, so she missed him during each weekday for about the first 520 weeks of her memory. Then for about the next 520 weeks, she hardly saw him at all. He disappeared not only from her, she gathered, but from himself. She collected sharp little shards of his life from these years, like this story's lesson in irony: someone shot at him (though, thankfully, they missed) at the *Friendly* Inn. Otherwise, these became the "don't ask me about those times" years. Once, during that period, he'd called his daughter in the middle of the day—unaware that these were school hours, and she was skipping them—as she lay in bed with her high school boyfriend, the LSD nearly worn off the neurons, regrettable sex and orange juice sticky on her mouth, to hear her father say he still loved her mother. Laughing at love's futility all these years later, writing it off as his own drunkenness talking. "Dad, you're funny," said the drugs. Father and daughter always had so much in common.

CONSEQUENCES

For the first ten years of my life, my father bought a new book for me every time I saw him on the weekends. Each visit he'd read a novel, sometimes two, as I read next to him, pointing at each word as I clopped along. *Don Quixote was one funny, lascivious fuck*, he once said. I wanted to hold such opinions. The consequence is that I grew to be a reader and wanted to be just like him.

In the early 1970s, before they were my mom and dad, both worked at Maison Blanche—she in the women's department, he in furniture. One May evening he approached her for help looking for a present for his mother. She was charmed. She asked which style his mother preferred, what her size was. My father said, "Style? She's parachute-sized." My mother, despite herself, was even more charmed. The consequence was that they went on one date and another and eventually moved in together and broke up and reunited, in the same cycle of not-so-well-matched but physically attracted partners. Then they got married, and despite his insistence on the ruinous nature of everything, that bringing children into the world is tantamount to cruelty, they were elated by her unplanned pregnancy, and subsequently, I was born. The consequence was that they were both changed, though as with most parents, not in the ways they expected. The consequence, one of very many, was that I grew up and became a writer and wrote this essay.

Noon on that fall day. It's sunny. We decide we don't want to go home yet. We drink Abita Andygators and split a burger at the new Chelsea's under the overpass. Drunk, we leave our car there and walk home. Brock says the leaves, the dead ones, are the color of my eyes. We unlock both deadbolts and lie down on the couch, turn on the TV to watch the 700 Club. My father isn't home. He's probably out buying us ginger ale and renting the latest Disney/Pixar film, like he always does. My father lives, and lives with us, forever.

SECOND-PERSON FUTURE PERFECT

Sometime in it you will have been long gone, as will everyone you have ever loved. Whether you'll have chosen God or the worms, there will still be so much of the *not this* there. No more stories, no more hearing from your father and not having been heard by him, all of which you will have missed, until the worms (or God) will have come for you. But until then, you will have created and repeated new stories that will have lived in different incarnations.

But before the worms, your father will have visited your home for the first time in eleven years. Different doorway, couch, television, room, city, father, daughter. By then, you'll have been more mother than daughter. Your father, by then a grandfather, will have weighed two pounds less than he did eleven years before. You'll know because he'll have told you. You will have weighed fifteen pounds more, though you won't have told him (or needed to). Your husband will have weighed the same and will have remained respectfully distant during the visit. He will have known to cede this time to the ones who needed it most.

You and your father will have watched your two-year-old daughter play on the floor—discrete puzzle pieces in her hand, puzzle board missing, possibly under the couch, though none of you will have cared to look. Your daughter: much more enamored with these pieces than the prospect of fitting them together into a larger whole. You will have wondered: what will happen when she anticipates the pieces making up a whole? And before it's all over, what will she have done with the pieces of your story you'll have given her? How much will have been too much to offer, or too little, or just enough, and how will you ever have known the difference?

One afternoon during the visit, two wine spritzers deep, your father will have said *you have a nice life*, and the way he'll have looked slightly above your head, to someplace that only he has access to, suggests he will have meant it in past/present/future tenses. At some point he'll have placed his feet up on the ottoman, and you'll have been so happy he's comfortable (though you'll have wondered, and hate yourself for having wondered: *is he getting too comfortable?*). And you'll have been silent once again in the knowledge of all you don't need to understand. You'll have loved him, and known him, and not known him, in all the tenses. You won't have had to say a word.

NICE LADY

At times it's been hard to think about this story and like myself, which is probably why I've always played with the details. Because it happened, but not in the way I would've preferred it to. Because making meaning of it involved projecting onto myself not just brownness or whiteness, wokeness or brokeness, wrongness or rightness, but some muddled, middle version that makes any self-narrative more challenging to share.

What happened was this: early Tuesday morning of May 6, 2008, in Baton Rouge, Louisiana, two young Black men carjacked my husband and me three weeks after we were married. My purpose in telling this story, back when I loved to tell it, was that I wanted the audience to affirm what I wasn't so sure of. I was a good person, resilient in how I handled near tragedy with aplomb. I wanted my audience to laugh at details I incorporated, like how I was wearing four-inch Kenneth Cole heels, fake mustache stuck to my pants, while running for my life. I wanted to fascinate them with what's difficult by making it sound not difficult at all.

Back then, a strong compulsion for telling the story was that if there were such a thing as good or bad victims, I would've been an A+ gold-star victim. At the time of the carjacking I'd been canvassing for Obama's first presidential election, proudly brandishing his *¡Sí Se Puede!* bumper sticker on my car; I shared my love of Baldwin and Wright with the American literature undergraduates I taught at Baton Rouge Community College; and I am, after all, the daughter of an Ecuadorian immigrant, so my people have endured our share of racial oppression. Ideally, crimes like this happen to no one, but in a slightly righteous world, a more appropriate victim might be one of the many open racists I've met throughout my life living in the Deep South. My former landlord, for example, to whom we'd later tell of the carjacking one night over dinner, whose eight-months-pregnant wife first asked the race of the carjackers, and then, face hardening, blurted that most infamous racial epithet to punctuate the story, as if that word was the simple lesson to be learned, then wiped her mouth of mayo from the burger we'd cooked and served her. I've heard that word my entire life, and though extended family members have learned not to use it around me, I've never had courage enough to tell acquaintances or near strangers to fuck off when they've used it. I've told myself that moralistic admonishments won't help the antiracist cause, but honestly, I wanted to avoid confrontation. In the face of the n-word, I've often looked away. But I'd show this woman! She was never invited to my home again. The next time I saw her was in my mind's eye, as I conjured her for this essay.

When telling the carjacking story aloud, I've often left out intricate details: how the night was balmy, like walking through cotton candy without its sweetness, and more materially, the carjackers held us at gunpoint on the corner of Aster and Nicholson, just as we left a friend's Cinco de Mustache, a party name I blithely ignored at the time but flinch at in hindsight, where velvet, stick-on mustaches were available at the door. None of these mostly white academic friends with whom we later shared the carjacking story would ever, ever use the n-word—in fact, I'd heard a Hegelian harangue or two from white colleagues declaring that no one, including Black people, should ever say it, since now was long past the point of reappropriating it for power. Nor did our good, progressive friends ask about the carjackers' race, because it didn't matter. What mattered was we were safe, and hey, now we had a story to tell.

Have I mentioned this is also a story about race?

In writing this story, I should underscore the soundtrack involved: Mos Def's song "Mathematics" from his 1999 album *Black on Both Sides*. Now known as Yasiin Bey, Mos Def was then the kind of socially conscious hip-hop artist that a half-Latina, half-white, Nice-Liberal Person like myself would listen to. Whereas a rapper like Kanye reminds us in each refrain of his own genius, Mos Def says: the inequities of the world are on everyone, so wake the fuck up. Listening to him, I felt evolved. I can't remember exactly what part of the five-minute song I heard when the men first approached my car on the night of May 6, but retrospectively the lines set in relief speak to the ruthless math so many young Black men confront when they're no longer faces, just lines and statistics.

Those lines find further meaning in the context of a 2008 Baton Rouge that was 55 percent Black and 40 percent white after Hurricane Katrina, a demographic flip-flop after many Black New Orleanians living in the Ninth Ward and New Orleans East were flooded out of their homes and sought refuge in the closest large city to the north. A few years from now, a group of white residents in the more affluent southern portion of Baton Rouge will petition to create a new city named St. George, with the more preferable 70 percent white and 23 percent Black configuration. That the 2015 petition failed by seventy-one votes out of a total of nearly eighteen thousand suggested the wealthy white voters would try again and again until they reached their preferable racial equation, a sainted city they could call their own. (On October 12, 2019, my thirty-ninth birthday, St. George was successfully incorporated as its own mostly white, tax-dollar-controlling entity.)

Back in my car after Cinco de Mustache, I'm sitting in the driver's seat and listening intently to the music, when two Black men approach my husband and our friend chatting outside my car. And I distinctly remember thinking: look how *not scared* you are right now, with Black men approaching you after midnight in an unfamiliar neighborhood. *You're a good person.*

Months after the carjacking, I moved to Tuscaloosa, Alabama, for a teaching job and promptly joined a race relations group. We called ourselves the Tuscaloosa Race Relations Initiative, or TRRI. The lawyer turned stay-at-home mom who brought us all together, Laurie, recruited us by finding our email addresses and ethnicities off a Democratic Party mailing list, and what this group did, essentially, was discuss race. Eventually our goals were to recruit forward-looking city council representatives and desegregate Tuscaloosa County schools, but we didn't get much past the talking. In fact, local school segregation worsened in the years after our formation. In her May 2014 *Atlantic* article "Segregation Now," Nikole Hannah-Jones posits that the Tuscaloosa public school system is more segregated now than at any time since the landmark *Brown v. Board of Education* Supreme Court ruling, because in 2000, a federal judge released city schools from the desegregation mandate. As a result, one in three Black Tuscaloosa children attends a public school that looks like *Brown v. Board* never happened. Hannah-Jones refers to these as "apartheid" schools. One of them is a mile away from where my husband and I bought our first home in 2015. Supposedly progressive white colleagues in our neighborhood had slowly begun moving away from our poorly rated school district—71 percent Black, 21 percent Hispanic, and 6 percent white, with a 1/10 greatschools.org score—because, well, these were mathematics not even nice people could abide. *Not us*, my husband and I repeated like mantras, *our kids* will go to the public school where we live, where there's affordable housing *and* racial diversity, a school that lacks decent test scores but provides us a chance to get involved and make it better. We'd say this, I see now, behind the relief valve of not yet having children.

TRRI would solve none of these issues, but we would get to know one another pretty well through our stories (though we were more likely racial and ethnic totems to one another). A calculatedly diverse group, some of us, including me, seemed a little too proud about that. Counted among us was a Militant Ex-Felon, a Black Woman Nurse, an Asian Woman Journalist, an Earnest White Bookseller, and a Peevish Black Plumber. To my chagrin, in the mostly white academic circles where for two decades I've kept my company, friends have generally identified me more with the white side of my half-ness, but within this group, or at least according to Laurie, I was the Latina English Professor. I mention TRRI because it was during one of these meetings that I was first publicly shamed about my carjacking story. I told it because we'd been asked to share an experience in which race played some complicated part. By then I'd told the story many times, but finally, here was the audience who could more deeply chew on it.

So I told it, placing emphasis on the thought I'd had just before we were carjacked, which I'd subsequently realized was misguided, but in that moment had prided myself on: look how *not scared* you are, *you're a good person*. Leading up to this revelatory moment, I included all of the Obama/Mos Def details because they even further showed my ineptitude, the insane idea that loving Black culture would safeguard me from violence or crime. But as I concluded my story, Jerry, the Peevish Black Plumber, asked, "Why did you do that?"

"Do what?"

"Listen to rap like that? You trying to impress those boys? Trying to be cool?"

This was turning into the type of interrogation that both the police and insurance investigator had spared me after the carjacking, and I didn't appreciate it. Who the hell was Jerry?

"Jerry," I said. "I didn't listen to it for their benefit."

"Yeah, but I'm trying to picture what you're saying. You're a white girl. You see Black dudes. So even though you were already listening to the music, now you were doing it *for them*. You're trying to prove to them you're cool, you're down."

"Well, maybe I am cool," I offered. Nobody laughed.

"And I'm not white," I whispered, peevish as Jerry, and though no one heard me, I regretted it. Who was I to argue with a Black man about race, even if it's my own?

The truth was I wanted Jerry to be okay with me. I'd hoped that by pointing to my own ignorance before anyone else could point it out, I'd absolve myself of that very ignorance. But Jerry wasn't having it. All this took place years before embodying *wokeness* became the ultimate virtue signal of the American Left, but Jerry sniffed out early in me that cloying liberal guilt, which doesn't self-erase by sheer admission. The sardonic lessons from the 2017 film *Get Out* weren't yet part of our lexicon either, but I can imagine Jerry now having seen that movie and thinking, "mhmm." White people loving (and envying) Black culture so much they're willing to entrap its people, literally steal Black souls to inhabit their superior, more talented bodies. The film resonated with me anyway: early on, wealthy, white patriarch Dean Armitage, speaking to his daughter's Black boyfriend, gushes over Obama, his love so cathectic that he never wanted the president to leave office, would've voted him in for a third term. While I wouldn't have said this to a Black or any other acquaintance (Armitage's "third term" line plays as cringeworthy earnestness), I share that sentiment with the villainous white character. I, too, cathected to Obama, and I suspect it wasn't only the politically right and center Obama supporters who felt their vote for him meant something deeper about themselves, that they were now inured from racial animus of any kind. But these thoughts do not inspire hope and change; they aren't thoughts for polite company. Around the time I told TRRI the story, I stopped talking about the carjacking so much, instead writing down the changing story and my changing role in it.

That I was silently polite in response to Jerry's grousing also proves to me that he was right: I was too intimidated to rhetorically push back against a Black man, who clearly had the expertise on all ideas regarding race (and yeah, how condescending is that?). But I do wish I'd told him that I was parts right and wrong, that we all have the potential to hold two opposing ideas at once. And the truth is I first learned about cognitive dissonance in 1993, the idea if not the term, from Tupac Shakur's single "Keep Ya Head Up." The song, an anthem to America's impoverished women, includes two oppositional sentiments lines apart from each other: that Shakur's mother sacrificed everything to raise their family, and that he blames her for making his brother a crack baby. Both then and now, right-wing news outlets have pointed to this problem with rap: its vilification and exploitation of women and also its intellectual inconsistency. How could a man in one breath lionize his mother and then condemn her in the next? But of course one could. One could be a criminal *and* a loving person. A do-gooder *and* a fuckup. I wanted Jerry to know this about me—that rap was part of my formative ideology, and while I can't fully understand the centuries-old devastation imposed upon Black people by white people, I've always tried pushing back against the injustices. I'm politically active. I listen to Black friends and acquaintances like Jerry about what we should do to improve racial matters, which seem to-day—a decade later, with the resurgence of a Trumpian white nationalist movement and the brutal killings of unarmed Black men by those who purport to protect and serve, as much a primal white scream as the one heard during the Montgomery bus boycotts and Jim Crow repeals—to be *the* central issue to solve in contemporary American culture. And though we might speak out on social media, call out dog whistles and blackface yearbook photos, read the indispensable words of Ta-Nehisi Coates and Tressie McMillan Cottom, carry signs to our peaceful protests, I still fear we are imperceptibly getting worse, not better, at dealing with race. We all seem to be running furiously in place.

Though this entire paradigm hadn't yet made itself known during my discussion with Jerry (the Tea Party was beginning to trumpet its "our political concerns are definitely *not* driven by race lol" fanfare), I knew enough not to argue with him about race: his, mine, or their places in the public consciousness. Because as Toni Morrison writes in *Playing in the Dark: Whiteness and the Literary Imagination*, it's a gracious, liberal gesture to ignore race. To either genuflect or disagree with a Black man about it? Well. Nice, liberal, part-brown, part-white women don't do that.

Days after my Baton Rouge carjacking, an insurance agent called requesting I meet with him about my "unfortunate incident" before the agency could cover my losses. Tyler the State Farm agent looked like one of the undergraduates I taught, spiked blonde hair with a soft voice and hands, and that felt about right, because to meet him I dressed in my best teaching outfit: black slacks and a black-and-white pin-striped Gap top. I even wore my silver-buckled black belt, which meant, I meant business. In my nervousness, though, two circles of sweat soaked under the arms of my blouse. I jutted forth my forearm to shake Tyler's hand.

As I adjusted in my chair, trying to find my most trustworthy-looking seating position, annunciating in my most formal teaching voice how grateful I was for his time and assistance, Tyler stopped me before I could speak of my "incident," and I still remember his speech almost verbatim.

"So, Miss, what this meeting is supposed to be about, we don't have to do. My job here is to make sure your unfortunate incident isn't part of some insurance scam, or something else. Unfortunately, we have to do that a lot in this business—make sure people's stories check out. But I could tell right when you walked in that you're a nice lady, that something truly terrible happened. If you want to tell me about it, that's fine, but you don't have to. Whatever you like."

I recounted some version of the story I'd come to tell many times in the future, but couldn't focus on his sincere head nods because I began wondering: Why such latitude with me when other claimants were forced to provide extensive documentation and testimony proving their claims? What made me reflexively *nice*? My presence was the evidence he needed, with all the socioeconomic and racial viability it suggested. To Tyler, I was a well-dressed, well-educated, trustworthy white woman. This is the kind of inequity that comes from a privilege I'm ashamed of, and which might sicken TRRI members like Jerry, which was probably why I didn't later share with them this part of the story.

Tyler's automatic acceptance reminded me how often my bifurcated racial identity plays in my favor. It calls to mind Du Bois's idea of the African American double consciousness with which, after first reading and teaching it in graduate school, I've always identified. But my double consciousness works differently. It holds the added guilt that rather than the doors of opportunity always being closed off, people in my orbit often project onto me whatever color makes them the most comfortable. Black and brown female colleagues from various provinces of my work history—women working at law firms, as data entry coders; in restaurants, as servers; in universities, as professors—will confide in me, as a fellow woman of color, their racist interactions. White female colleagues in these same work environments see me as brown enough to use as a resource for their racial curiosities. But they also see me as someone who isn't too hung up on all that race stuff, because, let's face it, I'm part-white, so how hard could it be for me? As far as they can tell, I'm pretty much one of them. With everyone, I'm always welcome.

When Jerry the Plumber later called all this into question, I interpreted him as saying, "tell us who you are—how *you* really see yourself." And I couldn't answer, either because I didn't yet know or was too scared to say. I can't remember which.

Another fuzzy carjacking story detail: meeting with police to identify the carjackers. I recall little about our visit to the Baton Rouge Police Department off Scenic Highway 61, except that detectives showed my husband and me pictures of far too many Black faces. One mustachioed detective jabbed at the broad jaw lines of two particular Black men. He suggested these could be—*should* be—the perpetrators. "They're wanted for vicious crimes, and it would be super if you could testify against them."

When I said, "I don't know. I tried not to look at their faces," the officer said, "Please." He sighed heavily. When we left after giving them nothing, they seemed disappointed.

Later I wondered how much I would've contributed to the conviction of two supposedly dangerous Black faces I didn't recognize if I'd said *fine, okay, maybe it was them.* Taken the attitude of, it's business, no faces, only lines and statistics. If the detectives would've coached me in their convenient version of who was responsible, or if they'd insisted I recant if I wasn't sure. What they'd have considered justice.

This part of the story is harder to tell, and to write, which is why I never have.

I don't know their faces, but I remember their voices. They snatched my purse containing my wallet and debit card, but most importantly the handwritten note from Deuce McCallister, former New Orleans Saints running back, procured by my stepfather the night before my wedding at our Drago's rehearsal dinner on Poydras, that read something poetic like, "enjoy your journey of meals and days together, always set your table nice." I almost asked the carjackers if they would allow me to dig through my purse to find the note, but then they started shoving me back and forth between them, so I stayed quiet.

"Pop her," one said. "You pop her!" the other responded. These two words punched out on the page don't do justice to the terror they inspired at that moment.

To tell a story aloud is not to tell the truth of it, because some moments you have to hold. *Pop her*, and what that meant. How I hoped in those few seconds of terror, despite knowing better, that "pop her" meant rape, and not kill.

Over the years I've told the carjacking story many times, but there have always been two different versions, depending on how much I trust my audience, and the untrue version at some point became more real to me than what actually happened.

What actually happened: after leaving the Cinco de Mustache party, even though I was recovering from a late-spring flu, we agreed to our friend P.'s offer to score us some blow and keep the party going. P. knew someone who knew somebody else, and this somebody agreed to meet P. around the corner. My husband and I waited in the car outside the party, listening to *Black on Both Sides*. After enough time passed to realize this wasn't worth the wait, I said, "Let's go home." We drove around the block and there was P., talking to not one but two somebodies against a white stucco apartment building. I pulled into the parking lot and said to myself, *I'm not scared, I'm a good person*, and my husband jumped out, offered P. and the two guys a cigarette, and then before anyone understood what was happening: *gimme that purse, pop her, no you pop her*.

Yet when I remember *them* approaching *us* after we left the party, asking my husband for a cigarette, asking what was up for the night, I see that version perfectly too. But it never happened that way. We inadvertently pulled up to the danger. Afterward, we felt foolish, ashamed for getting caught up in a drug deal we weren't even particularly interested in. This wasn't how good, liberal people like us defined ourselves—by this stupid little event that, according to our perpetrators, could have ended in a pop. So it was regular old color-blind shame that prevented me from telling the whole truth all this time.

But before shame or acknowledgment of our stupidity, there was getting our stories straight. They wore blue jeans. Had black skin. One shorter and stockier, the other like a string bean. Young men. Likely not yet twenty. We were on our way home from a party. *They* approached *us*.

All but the last three words are true. With a transposition of pronouns, a drastically different story. Or is it? How is it that I always get to play the hero, both when I admit the truth and when I don't?

The racial and liberal guilt and purported lack of fear and then great fear were also true, but no one to whom I've ever told the story wanted to hear about all that.

Another story I've told myself from time to time, in daydream: the carjackers and I have a conversation in our mutual rap language. Through Jay-Z's "Blue Magic," they defend their motivations that night, blaming Reagan and Ollie North for the failed, faux war on drugs that placed so many young Black men like themselves in the position to sell to begin with. And ruing my struggle to tell the story, I speak through Eminem's "8 Mile," lamenting I should quit writing since I'll never get it right.

I also recognize these daydreams, while true, are yet another virtue signal to my audience—you—that I'm educated *and* down. I can access the academy's language *and* the streets'. That even subconsciously, I embody cognitive dissonance. If I got the chance to talk to Jerry again, I'd finally give him an answer: I see myself as part authentically good person, part improvisor, part phony who wants every story she tells to be loved.

By 2020, twelve years after my carjacking, and despite the maelstrom of racial tensions burbling up between police violence and the public, despite Trumpism's interconnectedness with the darkest parts of this country's past, I've grown more hopeful. Though I despise the term "woke," we do seem more awake now than ever before. Protestors of all colors march along with their friends, with their children, to proclaim that this country as we've inherited it will not stand. Yet, with every contribution to the ACLU or NAACP or Bail Project, I retain the creeping anxiety that what our collective donations and protests reveal more than anything else is not the ostensible plea for true racial reconciliation, but the individual insistence on innocence. "See?" the white people's signs secretly chant, "*I'm* one of the good ones. *I'm* on the right side of history; you can trust *me*."

That desire for innocence is, in essence, what this essay has become, despite my wish that in admitting my shame, it would be more noble. It's what we're all likely to say when we admit what we believe to be the truth about ourselves. "I'm trying hard, so that makes me a good person."

It's another fear of mine that won't unstick. In confessing the truth, I'm worried that even if I'd told all authorities and every audience who has ever heard this story the whole truth from the beginning, they—you—still would have thought my role in it was all okay. You would have found some version of *nice lady* to confer onto me, laud me for my honesty, then divert your attention to other, more convenient faces as part of the real problem. White guys in red hats, white officers kneeling on blameless necks, Black guys with guns. *You're fine*, you'd say. *You're a nice lady*. Because after all, I've tried so hard to be honest, to be a good person, reveal my shame . . . so aren't I one?

≫→ ≫→ ≫→ ≫→ ≫→ ‹≪ ‹≪ ‹≪ ‹≪ ‹≪

PART III

TWO LIES
AND A TRUTH

COMEDY OR
TRAGEDY?

≫→ ≫→ ≫→ ≫→ ≫→ ‹≪ ‹≪ ‹≪ ‹≪ ‹≪

(1) As a writer, I operate under a tragic framework.

Shit, let me back up and explain what that means.

Twentieth-century rhetorician Kenneth Burke devised theoretical frameworks for how people interpret the world, using poetical terms and symbols to describe basic attitudes toward human experience. Two frameworks are set in opposition to each other. One is tragic: events are understood through their most fatalistic prisms. When bad things happen, that's because human motives are intentionally vicious. In this paradigm, people are typically seen as victims or villains, and equanimity is found through a scapegoat who is sacrificed, thus purifying the social order. The tragic framework's major drawback is its intense earnestness and self-pity. Then again, clear categories offer simple answers, and in a world this nuts, simplicity can be a relief.

Burke searches back to the Romans to support his thesis about the curve of history, and why different frameworks arise during the contexts of different eras. I'm partial to the Greeks, though, and in particular their muses (I wore my necklace bearing Calliope, muse of poetry, as a talisman while writing this. I'll leave it for you to decide if she worked). Barthélemy Lafon, eighteenth-century Creole architect, was also a fan of the Greeks, which is why he designed New Orleans neighborhoods in the Greek grid style and named nine of its streets after the Nine Muses. Melpomene, muse of tragedy, plays the lyre, which, frankly, is a turnoff. (All that bring-bring-briiiiiiinging is not for me. If you've never heard the lyre, explore "lyre-playing" on YouTube and you will promptly discern why music is no longer taught in public schools.) Anyway, despite my operating under the tragic framework, Melpomene is not the muse I'd go for.

Still, she's worthy of further examination. Melpomene, the street in New Orleans, is located in the lower Garden District. I pass it every time I take my kids to Boo at the Audubon Zoo for Halloween, usually stopping first at Juan's Flying Burrito on Magazine for a mind-erasing, fourteen-dollar margarita. Melpomene (the street, not the muse) has the distinction of being included in Ricky B's 1994 Nola classic bounce song "Shake Fa Ya Hood," which contains the catchiest refrain I'd ever heard as a thirteen-year-old: "Shake for your mother-fucking hood if it's good / fuckin right it's all right / fuckin right it's all right." This song was written when New Orleans was considered one of the murder capitals of the country (a dubious merit it garnered once again in 2022) and includes the lyrics: "Slugs coming at your ass, nigga, duck bitch duck / And you can't do shit because you're cornered in the cut." In this song, systemic racism is the villain and the scapegoat; the young Black men of New Orleans killing each other because they've been taught to believe there's a difference between "third ward, ninth ward, tenth ward, sixth ward" are the victims. As Ricky B tragically laments, "All y'all [caught up in this system] do is make shit hard." Still, it's a bounce song, so there's the inherent hope that what might right the social order is singing (and bouncing) instead of slinging.

But back to Lafon, who could not have imagined a future Ricky B or what the streets of his beloved Melpomene would see. Lafon seems to have led a double life, both as an esteemed architect/engineer and a depraved smuggler. He was known to have side-hustled with infamous pirates Pierre and Jean Lafitte. This surprising bifurcation leads naturally to the next Burkean framework.

(2) As a writer, I operate under Burke's comic framework.

Through this frame, one achieves understanding, or hopes to produce societal or personal change, by poking fun at the faults and flaws in the system (or the self). When bad things happen, that's because human motives are inadvertently mistaken: not vicious, nor evil, just stupid. What I love most about this framework is the near constant recognition of the human propensity toward idiocy. If you fuck up, or don't know the answer, or change your mind, good! You're *supposed* to get it wrong, you're *not supposed* to know! Yet there's a nasty cynicism that can develop under the comic frame, when everything is such a joke that there's no longer hope. In which case, I summon the muse.

Thalia, muse of comedy, is commonly depicted wearing a crown of ivy, heavy looking boots, and a comic mask. She's got the sort of alt-nineties, Dr. Martens-boot-wearing vibe I comically tried and failed to emulate as a teen (tragically, because we could not afford Dr. Martens). Thalia, the street, is located in the B. W. Cooper neighborhood in New Orleans, which I've spent no time in, and as far as I'm aware, is not depicted in any rap lyric.

(3) As a writer, I operate under both tragic and comic Burkean frameworks.

I, like Lafon, possess an identity bifurcated by the vastly different people who made me. For example, consider how my father responded to the immediate aftermath of Hurricane Katrina. He was working as a steward on an offshore boat when his crew got word they needed to return to shore immediately because this hurricane was going to be The Big One. They docked early Sunday, and Katrina hit early Monday. The next forty-eight hours were absolute chaos as he tried to find a place to stay, since his neighborhood was under mandatory evacuation (all he knew for sure: fuck no, *not* the Superdome). But even as he was experiencing this trauma, he was already figuring out how to convert it to comedy. Like when a pretty pit bull followed him down Canal, where my father was looking for someone with a vehicle whom he could pay to drive him out of New Orleans—north, east, or west, didn't matter to him. The pit bull nuzzled my father's legs, which made him feel special, and he wondered if this dog was the last real connection he'd make in the world, till he remembered the beef jerky in his pocket. When he finally looked into the dog's eyes, the dog said, according to my father, "motherfucker, *feed me*."

Then, there was Lala's reaction to Katrina. She evacuated with my mother, stepfather, and four sisters to stay in the home Brock and I had recently rented in Baton Rouge. Not even one drop of rain—*ni una gotita*—fell on her head. An hour northwest of New Orleans, we got some wind, some tree limbs down, and, disturbingly in the Louisiana swelter, lost electricity for a few days. But then our power returned, meaning we had television. Lala proceeded to suffer several breakdowns over the next few weeks, over *ese cara de verga* (dickface) Bush. *Por ese* who did *nada para nadie*, for the poor people wading through water with televisions. Who could blame them for trying to get something after they lost everything? One afternoon shortly thereafter, breaking news showed footage of a midflight 747 with faulty landing gear dumping most of its fuel into the Pacific to prepare for a safer crash landing. We awaited the fate, between long commercial breaks, of its nearly two hundred passengers. This was more than Lala could bear. She offered Valium to everyone in the house, including my dog. "Everything is hopeless," she said. "Even planes don't know how to fly anymore, and not even *Diosito* can help us now!" When not even God is on your side, you're in a classic tragic framework.

Thus, while I carry both tragic and comic impulses within me, I prefer a messy mixture of the two. I prefer *buggy*. My muse for this paradigm is my dog King, who died of a broken heart (also, old age) a few months after his sister, Nola, was hit by a car. He was both a practical boy who dutifully licked the sleep out of Nola's eyes but also lovingly licked away our human tears over the world's tragedies. He's the only dog I've known to both genuinely smile and smirk. He observed his subjects (often me) deeply, and he understood me, or tried to. He simply loved and loved simply. My goal is to observe as thoroughly as he did, to generally be more like him. If I could find a way to replace Calliope with him, wear a part of him as a talisman around my neck, I wouldn't hesitate. I think I've kept a pouch of his toenail clippings around here, somewhere . . .

BUGGINESS

I haven't seen or spoken to her in months, but tonight, my sister Alexa needs me to give her a ride to Lipstixx strip club in the French Quarter, and I'm eager to oblige. More than wanting to help, I want to insinuate myself into her life, be a participant, be *needed*, and am inadvertently needy in that desire. She, on the other hand, seeks a job and doesn't have a car. Complicated, meet uncomplicated, though the stories behind who we are to each other, and why, entangle themselves from here.

We pull away from my mother's house on the Westbank of New Orleans, which is in some ways the aesthetic opposite of the French Quarter: here it's all concrete, strip-mall-y sameness. Residents rarely go downtown because everything that's great about this city—the rotten, stankin hotness off the pavement, even in winter; street kids affectionately known as Quarter Rats stoop sitting with sweet-faced pit bulls; a Smithwick's at the open window of Molly's in the morning if you feel like it, and you might as well feel like it, walking Decatur with go-cups of beer or an open flask because, hey, you can do that here—is anathema to suburban Westbankers. Better to get that seedy stuff on HBO. Work all day at a barely tolerable job, pick up fried chicken fingers for dinner with a side of crinkle-cut fries from Raising Cane's (their interstate billboard sign reads "West*Bank* on it!"), eat them on the couch while watching Game Show Network. For many Westbankers I know in the pop-up subdivision from which I spent my teenage years seeking an escape, it's that kind of life.

When in Nola, it ain't no thang to roll through the drive-thru of New Orleans Original Daiquiris and order a large Amaretto with an extra shot to start slurping on the way to your sister's stripper interview. I worked at a daiquiri shop years ago in college, around the time I began striving to rid myself of Westbank expressions like "ain't no thang." I don't remember my first daiquiri, but I remember Alexa's. On the way home from a Mardi Gras parade, I'd known the whole time that both my elementary-school-aged little sisters were surreptitiously sipping Mom's Jungle Juice from the backseat and pointing at each other's red-stained clown mouths. Rather than stop them, I let it go on because I was going to teach my sisters everything essential about the world, including how to drink, and the kinds of boys and drugs to avoid and to embrace and what it meant to be the right kind of girl, all of which I believed myself, in my fourteen-year-old wisdom, to be intimately familiar with.

Something else to know about Alexa at the time we're driving to the Quarter for her Lipstixx interview: she's nineteen and pregnant with her second child. What neither of us knows yet is that she'll spend the greater part of the next few years pregnant, giving birth to three sons before she turns twenty-two. Or that she and I will spend intermittent years between then and now estranged, for which I can place unequivocal blame on her in conversation with my friends, where it's easier to tell the valiant, false narratives about ourselves, but not here in writing, where I can see what I say.

During my first post–graduate school years teaching in Alabama, whenever the subject of my sister came up among colleagues, they asked reflexively if her children had different fathers. My impulse was to get all Westbank on them and say, "Aw nah, bruh, I wish those kids came from more than one dude, ya heard me! The father's a *Muslim* named *Christian*, and that shit ain't even funny cuz he's a fucking whackjob, ran her out they house naked one night beating her ass with a leather whip, threw our mom into a window during a heroin high, another time, swear to Christ, killed her dachshund Cocoa when he taped the dog's snout together, the sick fuck, and stuffed him in the garage refrigerator. Yeah you right, he's a piece a shit. All that mess and I ain't even started telling you stories, bruh."

But I don't talk that Westbank way anymore. Instead I tell my acquaintances that no, my nephews have the same father, and he's terrible, and I do not approve.

Alexa has the distinction in our family of saving our mother's life. In late 1990, when the blanket of pine needles I'd promised and then forgotten to rake covered our backyard, my mother, Rosita, five months pregnant with Alexa, came down with what she thought was the flu: high fever and vomiting for two days. When the vomit turned to blood, she checked herself into the hospital where the unpronounceable bacterial infection *Streptococcus pyogenes* was diagnosed. Necrosis followed rapidly, so Alexa was removed by Caesarian and incubated, and Mom's kidney dialysis and her circulation both failed. Rosita's memory of that time is a priest with halitosis read her the last rites. She doesn't remember that for several minutes the green line of the EKG remained flat, and then, it spiked. First, a blip. Then, a breath. Later, they said she'd recover mostly, but so much of her body's circulation had been impeded that her legs would have to be amputated at the knee. A few days afterward, it was determined only both feet would go, and, finally, after a recovery no doctors could explain, six and three quarter toes were removed. It took my mom nearly a year to learn her legs again and walk without the tiny balancing pads at the tips of her feet. She fully recovered, though her marriage to my sisters' father died a resigned death. He'd hardly visited her at the hospital. We heard later the word around the neighborhood was that he spent that time with friends at their ironically named favorite bar, Everybody's Here Too, weeping into his Rolling Rock about how much he was suffering. Before Mom could even walk again, she kicked his ass out. "Thank God he's gone," she said. "That marriage was killing me."

Up until my twenties, I believed Alexa had somehow caused Rosita's illness, that she'd bored a hole in her placenta or something. I wrote a poem in high school in which an evil black-eyed sister does this. Back then, I consoled myself with the knowledge Alexa was born with a face not even a mother could love: when Alexa was first brought to her, Mom shook her head and asked if the nurses had made a mistake. Being born so prematurely, Alexa was an undeveloped anthropoid, her body less fuzzy peach, more wiry rambutan. But, later, when I found out that this pregnancy saved my mom, that it was the sole reason Mom checked into the hospital that mid-November day when the strep was discovered (Jim Henson had died of the same affliction months before my sister's birth—he'd thought it was the flu too), I became jealous of my sister for the first, though not the last, time. How come Alexa gets to save mom's life and I don't?

Onward to Lipstixx, Alexa and I cross the westbound bridge of Crescent City Connection, the name for the twin cantilever bridges that take us to and from the city. It sounds paradoxical to be heading west when coming *from* the Westbank, but because of the Mississippi River's circuitous route through the city, that's how the geography works. As a kid, whenever we traveled eastbound to the Westbank to visit Mom's friends, I remember feeling sorry for the older bridge because it looked its ancient age—you could see the red rust, the dull yellow lighting, and everyone always saying, "Thank God for the new bridge," even though the two were supposed to be thought of as one entity: the Crescent City Connection. Soon enough I was thanking God for them too, when the CCC hejira'ed me away to college and graduate school and a life of my own. I had to get out because I didn't belong on the Westbank: the language I yearned to speak and thoughts I aspired to think wouldn't be bred there, and during the years I was away at college, my returns home were replete, in each of my sentences and actions, with this implication: *I'm not like any of you. I'm* better *than you.*

My half-sisters Aimee and Alexa, eight and ten years younger than I am, share a father, which I've always attributed to their closer connection and the unfair reversal of the typical older/younger sibling dynamic: for as long as I can remember, they picked on me. One summer they made up a language from which I was totally excluded, and they called me Kooba, which they later admitted was the palindrome for "a book." This discovery delighted me, my lifelong bookishness a quality I'd grown to admire (a bit too much) about myself once I got to college, to which Alexa responded, "Sttthip, if you like that name, then that's what's wrong with you." Embarrassingly, despite all I've revealed about Alexa's repugnant baby daddy, what burns me up the most about him is that she once told me I would never understand him because he was by far the smartest person she'd ever met. "*Beaucoup* smarter," she emphasized. "*Him?!*" I said, "and not . . ." "No," she said, "not you." And though she was clearly trolling my insecurities, that old comment stings even today. Alexa once fervently believed in the existence of the Illuminati; she's ping-ponged back and forth from Christianity to Islam, though the most ostensible difference, she finds, is the type of hot dogs she feeds her kids. Despite her protracted reliance on government assistance, and coming from a family of South American immigrants, she's pro-Trump in temperament and ideology, yet her opinion still means everything to me. This irony is not lost: her insistence that the abusive baby daddy is smarter than me has often made me want to punch her.

But see, I don't feel that Westbank way anymore. Now that my sister and I are adults, if not totally mature then at least on our way, I pine for small moments like these with her—this trip to the strip club—for some opportunity to trick her into following a certain set of prescribed steps (similar to the ones I took) for conjuring a better life: first flee the boyfriend and family, taking the new bridge away from the Westbank to anywhere; find something you love to do, then learn all you can about it; finally, learn to love yourself and wait for someone to come along and do the same, and *ta da*! You'll have a fulfilling life. Do as I did, and as I say. Right. Now.

Up ahead, I see the Tchoupitoulas sign, the first exit off the bridge, and I ask Alexa how long this "interview" will take. Hands off the wheel, I perform the air quotes with four fingers.

"Who knows."

"So, I have a question: do you think stripping is more about sexuality or capitalism?"

"What are you talking about?"

"Like whoever can screw—haha, screw—another person out of the most money is the winner?"

"Sttthip. I already told you, I'm not stripping." Alexa is an interminable teeth sucker.

"Oh, I forgot," I say, "you're applying for *greeter*." More air quote performance.

"Man, why you gotta be so stupid, Brooke?" But she's suppressing a smile.

We've crossed over the bridge, in more ways than one. I've been of several minds about this whole stripping/strip-greeter situation. For one thing, I don't see her performing sexuality in a convincing way. I mean, that's not any version I've ever seen in her. She's cute, compact, and utterly cold: her eyes, blacker than mine, betray no passions. I worry she'll fail at this job; yet I also worry she'll succeed. The minute she asked me for the ride, I began calculations of how much money she could make, which generously amounts to more than my advanced degree will earn me, and anyway I've bounced between severely underpaid teaching jobs since I graduated, so what is the brain worth, legitimately, when compared to the body? Not like in the grand scheme of things—but here, on the Westbank—truly, how stupid is what I do, trying to teach young people how to write when it's hard enough for me, when the very value of my body and brain— both supposedly A-one assets—are dubious?

But I can't say any of that to Alexa. I dump all of it down into the muddy Mississippi of my mind and tell her, "Well, let's define stupid. Your life is in my hands, and you're talking all this shit." Hands off the wheel again, I lace my fingers behind my head, easy-breezy, even though my knees inch up immediately to steer the wheel.

"Oh my god, you are so lame."

Alexa predictably rejects the newest version of myself, the lens through which I'm most fond of looking these days: the buggy way.

Bugginess comes, in part, from being born and bred in the briar patch of New Orleans. It's a word that represents for me the best of humanity: dogged, crazy optimism in times of darkness, an earned, post-Katrina perspective, a *flood-took-my-house-but-I've-got-a-full-flask* mentality. Its derivation was, in fact, a result of the hurricane, when our dog King seemed perpetually nervous yet, in his brilliant Australian shepherd way, smiled and nodded through the storm and the subsequent morass of family members turnstiling through our Baton Rouge home. My then-boyfriend Brock and I looked at him one day and said, "Buggy," and understood it. The word "buggy," it should also be noted, is what we New Orleanians call a shopping cart. When Brock, an Ohioan, first moved down here and heard that term, he loved the playfulness of what it connoted: that big thing that helps you move the smaller things you need to carry. It's no pedestrian "shopping cart"; it's a sweet, clanging buggy. So it was our dog, and grocery carts, that moved us to calling each other "buggy" as a term of endearment, as a way to love and be loved, and got me considering it as more than an uncommon noun, but a way to live.

The philosophy is simple: it's about not taking all this shit too seriously, all while still recognizing it's shit, and even loving the shit a little. It asks that we play this disastrous game of life with joy. It means when facing trouble, fear, confusion, both the minute and grand tragedies of our existence, rather than responding with self-pity, or horror, rather than letting it go or "it is what it is"-ing it, choosing to respond with a joke, some sarcasm, a story, to keep it going, to make even what's difficult a fond memory. It's a lagniappe of optimism in the larger gumbo of understanding, particularly when there sure-as-shit isn't any reason to remain optimistic.

Academically, the term bears similarity to the Nietzschean *amor fati*, or "love of fate," that promulgates an attitude in which one sees everything that happens in life, including suffering and loss, as good. Here, ignorance isn't bliss: knowledge is. Years ago, when teaching Milton in an early British literature course, I argued that the character of Satan, beyond being a classic example of the antihero, was the picture of bugginess: in his first lines, we see him cast down from heaven, and immediately he says, *Hey, this is hell, but it's not so bad.* And further, Satan puts a spin on this situation: *Didn't this battle I waged with God solidify his mightiness* ("till then who knew / The force of those dire arms?")? In other words, you're welcome for my betrayal, humanity: I, Satan, proved the existence of God. In trying to describe bugginess to students, I did not tell them (though it would have been buggy to do so) that the term stems from my surviving not only Hurricane Katrina but the Westbank—at one time, from my purview, a place far worse than hell. Now that I've referenced *Paradise Lost*, it follows that if Milton wrote his epic to justify the ways of God to men, then my much humbler work in this essay is to justify the ways of Westbankers to myself: and hey, that analogy is kinda buggy. So, a buggy scale: Milton's Satan = buggy. New Testament's Jesus = supremely kind and loving but too earnest to be buggy. Alexa = not even close. My mother = once she got into an argument with Alexa's baby daddy over the phone, and he thought he'd burned her by calling her a two-toed bitch, but then Mom said, "Oh, I've got four toes, motherfucker!" and hung up, went to the kitchen to make a sandwich. Buggy.

It's not an exact formula, since that kind of rigidity would be decidedly unbuggy, but in those early days of my marriage, escape from the Westbank still fresh, Shepard Fairey's *Hope* a new national symbol, it was a way to be. My struggle with bugginess, though, is that while it's easy to embrace, especially amid personal and political salad days, it's difficult to enact. Because how to avoid not wanting to retract, immediately, words or deeds you're not proud of? How to love everything about yourself—parts fearful, parts fulsome, parts phony?

Heading north on Decatur we pass Jackson Square. Andrew Jackson, bucked up on his horse, is often considered the defining symbol of New Orleans. He lost his entire family to maltreatment and disease before he reached manhood, so he had the suffering part down, and he saved New Orleans from the British, hence the seemingly unimpeachable statue, but his genocidal bona fides clearly rule out bugginess. And, at the far right corner of Saint Louis Cathedral, Muriel's Restaurant, another historic New Orleans landmark, where several years ago my husband and I were married (Muriel's Séance Room, where I drank a half-bottle of champagne before reciting my vows, is said to be inhabited by the ghost of Pierre Antoine Jourdan, a spirit who casts shadows and throws glasses across the bar, the very idea of which is buggy). Each moment of our ten-minute wedding ceremony and ensuing hours of drinking and dancing in the Small Plantation Dining Room overlooking St. Ann was perfect. Except: Alexa and I weren't speaking. And for some time leading up to our wedding, I'd been nervous Brock might see me differently, ever since he'd witnessed me go full-Westbank on that bee-otch.

Three weeks before the wedding, Brock and I had driven into Nola to pay the last of Muriel's deposit and tour its lush interior courtyard and wrought-iron wrap-around balcony one last time before our day. Then we took the old bridge to my mom's on the Westbank. Alexa, four months pregnant and eating a large Burger King meal at Mom's hexagonal kitchen table, was talking mad shit about Mom, who herself had been talking, according to Alexa, mad shit about Alexa's baby daddy. At first, I was annoyed by Alexa's litany of grievances, but the more she prattled on, impugning Mom's moral character, claiming that for the past seventeen years Rosita had been a total failure as a mother and human: *bla-dow*, I was Westbank-pissed, *ya heard me*. Added to my nerves was the fact that, for months, contrary to every one of my feminist impulses, I'd been severely restricting my calories in order to become bride-skinny, to create a body that eschews the fried-chicken-on-couch lifestyle of its forebears, and here my sister was allowed to be glowingly pregnant while eating an extra-large cup of fries. Even when she grew to nine months, she wasn't very big—Alexa had been a top-of-the-pyramid cheerleader, though her personality makes her more languid, like one of Eugenides's virgins (a simile, which given the context of her situation, you have to admit is funny). And oh, how languidly did she chew those fries. Because I was taking Mom's side in this discussion, and she noticed me noticing them, Alexa said, "Don't even think about it." She sucked grease from her thumb. I didn't want her gross food anyway, I said, telling her I couldn't understand her when she speaks Westbankese (score one for the buggy), but the problem was, I did understand, all too well. She spoke a language I couldn't unlearn.

As I sat across the table in an attempt to thoughtfully listen to her concerns, I saw it, a target: a wiry, white hair poking straight out of Alexa's head, a distinctive devil horn. All the women in my family go gray early, and this part of her, also a part of me, endeared her to me for a moment. It reminded me of the many times we'd popped each other's pimples or plucked each other's grays, picked through them like monkeys, according to our stepfather, helping each other root out what's amiss without the vicissitudes of language getting in our way. Just pure animal affection. It would have helped to know then what she was capable of—that a couple years later, after another vicious fight with her baby daddy, she will grab a pair of scissors, pull her hair from its ponytail and start chopping away . . . and that she'll call the police and accuse baby daddy of having cut it. For a long time and through an assortment of hair extensions, she'll let us all believe he did it—and why wouldn't he have committed this grotesquery, given his other crimes? But when she finally admits the truth, it will haunt me, how she had the temerity to strip her own beauty to enact revenge, that after so many transgressions—when he beat her or scared the babies and never paid a judicial price for it—she took justice into her own metal-sheared hands. The audacity. The insanity. The . . . *bugginess*. But in the before time, in the now of our argument, I was way past hair plucking: I wanted to yank her up by that thick black bun, dethrone her from her fast food kingdom. My mouth remained a tight line as she went on.

She said, "I ain't letting Mom see the baby, she keep it up."

She said, "I'ma tell this baby y'all wanted me to get an abortion, y'all wanted it to *die*."

She said, "Y'all bitches beaucoup crazy. I don't need this shit."

In the most mature version of the proceeding events, I, the self-possessed adult, say: "Alexa, trust me, I've been here. I railed against Mom when I was your age, and I thought she was the worst mother in the world. Then when I got to be a little older than you are, I thought she was the best mom in the world, that she could do absolutely no wrong. And now that I'm older, now that I'm at the perfect age and life situation to be advising you, I can see in hindsight that both suppositions are wrong. Mom is not the villain, or hero, but Mom: lovely and infuriating, always here when you need her to be, and annoyingly advisory even when you don't. She's good people, and she loves you more than herself." I could lay all of this out like a thesis statement with evidence and explanation to support. Use my words to gently guide.

In this version, Alexa listens intently as I explain, her dark eyes wide and focused, and says, "Fine, you're right." After she hands over a few fries, I employ the Rogerian approach to counterargue my own assertions by underscoring them with some buggy joke about what a pain in the tits Mom can be, coaxing Alexa further to my side, which is also, cunningly, Mom's side.

But it never works this way. When you see your old life passing before you again, you make the same old mistakes: all these years later, in my docile teaching town living my docile life, the fire pulses as I type this. There I am, that other me, separate from who I've become but reminding myself of what I'll do despite having known better: you'll morph into Westbank-you, you'll feel the appalling insufficiency of words, you'll seethe with the rage and fear of what you'd never be and what you are. You thought you'd left fear on that side of the Mississippi when you crossed over the new bridge for good. You didn't know you still lived with this rage.

I'm on fire. I'm about to lay hands on her in the same way men and boys who say they love us have done to us both, and to her, will again, and again. In that moment I don't stop to remember all the tender ways I've touched Alexa's face: in my Hitchcock phase, we laid in my bed watching *Vertigo* while I badly explained Laura Mulvey's theory of the male gaze, stroking her cheek. I've cupped her head in my hands when our stepfather drank and roared. I've kissed her *lunar perfecto*, the one that matches mine, except it's on her nose, kissed it because it was pretty, because Lala kissed mine.

But in this moment the past and future are of no consequence. I can't predict how badly I'll want to take this back, before learning, finally, to make fun of it, then let it go.

I still live with my Westbank rage, and my sister does too. I thrust two knuckles into her burger. She throws a handful of fries into my hair. We're both on fire. We both swing.

After our slap fight, after I'm married and two states removed and while Alexa's babies keep coming, as long as their father is out of the picture, our family back on the Westbank runs smoothly. I'm not bothered so much about my advice going unheeded because Alexa lets Mom help her now. "You know, Alexa's not being such a fucking idiot anymore," Mom insists. "Alexa says she's going back to school. Alexa's really trying to be a good mom. I think Alexa's finally got her shit together."

But for all that hope-and-change talk, this is how I find Alexa one evening during my summer break a couple of years later, when I stop by her apartment to pick up her basketsful of laundry for Mom to wash. The parking lot outside the St. Germaine apartment complex matches the building, matches the sky: all's gray on the Westbank that day, and a hard rain's falling, already several inches I slush through on my way in. As I pass Alexa's car, I notice her two front windows are halfway down. I open the door to 101-A, and as I wring out the black eel of my hair, I inform Alexa of her open windows, that she needs to roll them up. Both kids' car seats are inside, they'll get soaked.

"Duh," she says, "later." She continues texting. Then I look around. Juju, Son #2, crawls across the carpet, and surrounding him are about a hundred pieces of what appears to be steamrolled crap. That's the best description for these infinite brown, sometimes circular, sometimes square, sometimes tubular things. They're scattered around him like dirty Mardi Gras doubloons, and before I can fully register the absurdity of the scene, he picks one of them up and puts it in his mouth.

"Alexa, what in the fuck is that?" I point in disgust before I pick him up and swipe his mouth. He clamps my finger with his gums and smiles.

"Geez-um, it's grilled cheese. Sttthip."

I stop my swiping. "Well, how was I supposed to know that's a sandwich? It looks like you dumped out their diapers on the floor."

"Whatever."

"Yeah, whatever."

I turn to C.J., Son #1, who's eating macaroni and cheese one noodle at a time in his high chair, looking at me like I owe him money.

"Oh, hi, Buggy!" I say. More accurately, poor C.J. is unbuggy. He must know, even if he can't express it, that his terrible father once held him by the neck and told my sister that he could crush their world with one hard squeeze. In my anxiousness of what he's seen and has yet to see, I call him what I hope he'll grow to be.

"Sttthip, enough with the buggy!" Alexa says.

C.J. stares up at me. I offer a piece of macaroni, and he stretches away, which is when I notice he's naked in his highchair. Which, I can't say why (because I don't have children yet, thus am in the perfectly reasonable position to judge), freaks me out.

"Hey, Alexa, can we get a diaper on this kid or what?"

"He is wearing a diaper, Jesus!"

I reach into the highchair and feel for his naked baby bottom. He looks at me sideways, feeds himself another noodle.

"Dude, he's naked."

"No, he isn't, man, shut up!"

Now I'm feeling a little crazy. Didn't I just touch his bare ass?

I bend over with Juju still in my arms to check for C.J.'s nakedness under the front of the highchair. It's really important in this moment, in all moments, that I am correct.

And there I find, perched atop his naked baby penis, a cheesy macaroni noodle.

"Alexa, your son is naked, and you're letting him run around here with a macaroni dick."

She leans over to check and laughs. "Oh, huh. Well, anyway he's not running around; he's sitting quiet like a good boy. *You're* the one running around." She makes a kissing noise toward him, puckering her lips to the side. C.J. catches her kiss in his hand and blows it back, eats another noodle.

Juju is still gumming his floor food. I carefully flick away C.J.'s macaroni, and when I look back at Juju, he's got a perfect yellow cheese triangle hanging from his chin. Both boys are smiling and loving where they are, despite all evidence to what should be the contrary.

It's years after replaying and retelling this scene to friends and family, to myself, that I see what was always there. My sister, while not always easy to get along with, whose moods vacillate even more radically than mine, who at times has seemed deeply committed to blowing up her life, actually typifies bugginess more than I do. I wouldn't say she's buggy, but she's fine with being herself, whereas I'm constantly trying to change the both of us. *Amor fati*—she rolls with each of her new circumstances with acceptance, while I rewrite every scene, wishing I could have done it differently, parroting buggy without ever really embodying it. Bugginess is not, as I've often employed it, a way to measure myself against my sister. Bugginess is living in the moment with those I love without figuring out what lessons it can impart. It's kind of the opposite of what I'm doing right now, what I can never stop myself from doing. If being buggy is to both love and cut the shit, I can never quite cut it.

Idly, I drive up and down the streets of the French Quarter, past Checkpoint Charlie's bordering the Marigny, past Molly's on Decatur, back up the block-deep, palm-fronded courtyards behind the wooden doors on Chartres, down oak-lined Esplanade and past Royal's brightly lit art shops, waiting for Alexa to call me once her interview ends. At the northern edge of the Quarter, I remember the last time I passed this section of North Rampart, headed to the Central Business District and passing under the I-10 along North Claiborne. Mom and I were driving Alexa to Planned Parenthood sometime during her first first trimester. Under the overpass we saw one of Nola's many Tent Cities, where years after the storm, dozens of Katrina victims, still without homes or families to care for them, set up temporary canvas housing. In a moment so surreal I've often questioned its veracity, while we were stopped at a red light on Canal Street, a man emerged from one of the tents in a fine gray suit, holding a briefcase, ready for work.

Alexa said, "Ugh, what's wrong with these people? Why can't they find a real place to live?"

To which I said something like: *you spoiled little shit, it's because of Mom you have a home. It's because of us you're still okay.* The sound of silence after I get in the last word is the greatest victory, a temporary yet luminous salve that almost makes me forget there's a Tent City at all.

Alexa finally calls for me to pick her up, and I meet her at the Walgreens on the corner of Royal and Iberville. We chose this location because Alexa is the only person I know who doesn't understand the layout of the Quarter. It's a perfect grid. Bourbon doesn't curve and then become something else; it's a checkerboard of hedonistic simplicity that even I can't get lost in. I'd reminded her of this before she got out of my car, drew an emphatic square in the air. *Be more like me*, I wanted to say, *pay attention*, as she rolled her eyes at my exasperation: the old pot-and-kettle routine of sisters who, twenty years into their relationship, see each other more clearly than they see themselves.

When she climbs in, I say, "So, when do the boobies come out?"

"Sttthip, shut up. The manager left early. Gotta come back tomorrow night. Gonna need another ride."

"Happy to," I say, sipping the last icy chunk of my daiquiri. In thirty-six hours, I'll be back in my college town, in my grown-up roles as dedicated teacher and loving wife, a place where I won't drink and drive, and where I'll calmly cede my zero control over what Alexa does or who she becomes. But is there any bridge on Earth that can truly carry us away from the places we've lived and people we were? Intimations of my former self will continue to show up unexpectedly, reminding me I'm still a sister from the Westbank, figuring this shit out.

Crossing Canal on the way back to the I-10, Westbank bound, I ask Alexa if she remembers that suited-up dude with the briefcase in Tent City. I don't know what I expect to hear, but I'm surprised when she responds with this:

"Yeah, it sucked. That was beaucoup sad."

I don't ask why she feels that way now, or when she changed her mind, or if it was always sad to her. It's good to feel like she's growing, like we both are, maybe even closer, even if that's not true. What neither of us knows yet is that in a few years she'll cross the new bridge in her move to Houston, Texas, drifting further away from me, heading west to my east, that she'll give birth to two more sons, and then a daughter, that I'll have a daughter and nearly lose my mind in that first year of her life, crying many hours of the day and night over how little I know, despite all the books I've read, about sustaining a life, and nearly forgetting bugginess except as an idea of what I once desired and failed to be—I, who hardly recognized myself anymore.

I'll wonder during this time—the now time—if my sister still recognizes herself, and if she or I can ever admit to missing each other, these funhouse-mirror versions of ourselves. Ten years out from my bugginess heyday, with our national identity fractured, the easy proliferation of hate as a commodity, my personal and political salad days long gone, I'll wonder if the whole philosophy was a farce: isn't it easier to smile through the pain when we can predict its end, when the shared commodity is hope?

It's been over three years since Alexa and I said "hello" to each other, and I hardly remember our last goodbye. Reflecting on our relationship with real sincerity is buggy, I suppose—writing the essay displaying how I wished to be versus who I was to her, reckoning that there's no escape from who we've been. But loving and accepting her, despite all the ways we've hurt each other—that would be even buggier. These days I hardly even say "buggy" anymore. I just try to show it to my daughter, who already at two years old has a way of rolling her eyes that is somehow a parody of eye rolling, in a way I'm sure would make Alexa laugh. I may never have known bugginess, not the way I wanted to, but for now this memory feels good enough, this moment of connection one night when I did a small, kind thing: brought my sister to find work across the new bridge and then brought her home safely across the old one.

NOT THE LONELIEST COVER YOU COULD EVER DO

She first made herself known not through sight but sound. What did she sound like? Like a cartoon bubble bursting over my head. Like the bright *pop* sound Andy Williams makes in the chorus of The Chordettes' 1958 song "Lollipop," sticking his forefinger into his cheek and uncorking the champagne bottle of his mouth. Half-believing I dreamed the *pop*, I stood up from bed at 2 a.m. and felt a slow leaking, as if my body had forgotten how to hold itself together. At first I thought I was pissing myself. Then about a gallon of bloody water emptied from my vagina.

My daughter was due in almost a month, but she'd be arriving today. Still, I had reasons to remain calm. The hospital was one backroad mile from our home. My husband slept soundly next to my wet spot, but there was no need to wake him yet to pack a bag. I'd read that we wouldn't need to leave till contractions were four minutes apart, and that was likely hours away. All I needed was my phone timer and something to do. And I knew what that was. "Okay, this is good," I thought. "I have papers to grade."

It was the middle of the fall semester and I had subs to cover my classes, but I didn't want to leave them with a full set of ungraded memoirs. Besides, I like reading student memoirs. What's a "bad" one look like? Too self-centered? Too incomplete a narrative arc? Screw all that. My students share their lives with me. They may not completely plumb the depths of why things happen the way they do or what it all means, but they're getting there. They open up to me in ways they may not with their parents, in ways that—holy shit—my daughter might also close off to me someday. Yes, I was already this far afield while timing contractions and commenting on my students' uses of reflection and scene, entering grades ranging from A-minus to A-plus.

Then, I was somewhere twenty years in the future: who would this early girl be, and what would she mean to me. I couldn't imagine the answer; the question itself was terrifying.

In fact, the question required further distraction, so I scrolled through my DirecTV guide to where I usually find it: HBO. Paul Thomas Anderson's *Magnolia* had just started—a perfect movie for the desperation I was masking. Then, I was nearly twenty years in the past, first watching the movie and hearing the dial tone as the song "One" begins, *beep beep beep beep*. The singer leaned on the word "one" so deeply, so coolly, that it's the loneliest number a person could *do*. The opening film credits revealed a magnolia blossoming at hyperspeed, followed by the slow unraveling of depressed, lonely characters I would spend the next three hours paying half-attention to. Like I said, I'd seen them all before.

She first made herself known not through sound but sight. In my second year of college, my mom's best friend, Gloria, burned me a CD with a homemade cover design. She often made me gifts like this, introduced me to R.E.M. and Radiohead and all the Gen X coolness I'd always been slightly too young for. On this CD, a long, lanky woman, blonde and cool looking, like Gloria herself, wore a tankini and her name written in script across her body: Aimee Mann. Oh boy, I thought, another beautiful, blonde singer. But I trusted Gloria. She'd never married or had kids, so from my purview, her life composed of great-art consumption, astute political commentary, and believing in me. She cheered my amorphous writing ambitions, even masochistically asked to read early drafts.

Gloria wasn't an artist but loved art in all its forms. She could name all the architects who designed her favorite buildings in our hometown of New Orleans, and she was fun; she knew every rooftop bar in town. Because my mother spent much of her adult life raising three daughters, three stepdaughters, and cycling through three husbands, she didn't have as much time to slow down, pay attention. Whether or not a piece of art or music or film was beautiful didn't much matter. My mother rarely analyzed or let a thought or feeling linger. She accepted a breadth or dearth of beauty and moved on. At that time, in college, I saw in these two women two discrete paths for womanhood. The Gloria path was glorious. Freedom, one-ness, living life mostly for yourself. Though my mother is no martyr, I feared choosing her path would mean my own martyrdom. To be encumbered, constantly needed and tired, having little time to contemplate art and the self in the one life I was living. I needed time. I wanted to write, to make art, like this childless, beautiful Aimee Mann.

Because I wanted to impress Gloria, I didn't only listen to Aimee Mann, I studied her. I read somewhere that Anderson wrote the screenplay with Mann in mind, that he wanted his movie to be the equivalent of an Aimee Mann album. In that sense, the film was a cover of Mann's musical oeuvre established in the mid-nineties. The soundtrack's first song, "One," opens the film, and it wasn't immediately my favorite. The song contains no images. It's pure argumentative lament. When I first heard the album from start to finish, I was most gripped by the track "Save Me," probably because its narrator declares a nervous desire for a partner who fits with her, a girl in need of an emotional tourniquet. If you've ever really loved someone who's damaged, or been that damaged person, these are perfect opening lyrics.

Anyway, "One" is an ostensibly simpler song with simple lyrics. The relationship referenced is one where a presumed lover, or loved one, is gone. That's all we know. When I first heard it, the English major in me found it fascinating to hear that one was a number you could *do*. As in: enact, or perform. The rest of the song felt pointless to deconstruct. "One" is lonely; "no" is sad; yes, I get it. I remember sometime after Gloria burned the CD for me, I asked her what she thought of the song, to confirm if I was correct about it. She laughed and said, "Well, yeah, it's sad, but 'one' isn't *always* the loneliest number." Given that I planned to take her solitary path, I was glad to hear it.

Over the years, as I dug further into Mann's oeuvre, I learned

"One" was a cover with interesting tweaks to the 1968 Harry Nilsson original. Mann's version includes an electric guitar, and her tone makes the song's argument more starkly than Nilsson. He sings "one is the loneliest number" like it's a suggestion; when Mann sings it, "one's" loneliness is fact. But what I love most about the cover is how much Mann relies on Nilsson's voice, both at the track's opening and closing. In the opening, after the *beep beep* of the dial tone, we hear a male voice shout his readiness to sing to a "Mr. Mix." Which feels totally weird and nonsensical. Turns out it's Nilsson, from another of his tracks called "Cuddly Toy." And as "One's" final cryptic line concludes with the possibility of the number one being divided by two, Mann's voice recedes, and Nilsson's enters again. Here he sings lines not from "One," but more melancholy words about the impossibility of two people remaining together in a song entitled, appropriately, "Together."

I knew none of this when I obsessively listened to the soundtrack, but hearing a song titled "Together" superimposed over "One" is a bit ironic, and something that two decades ago, I could've written an A-plus paper about. Now, thinking about my relationship with Gloria, the song, and my daughter, who six years ago was in the process of being born as I listened to "One" while timing contractions, I'm considering the nature of covers. What makes a good cover? What should a cover song *do*? As in: enact, or perform. According to Ray Padgett's book on cover songs called *Cover Me*, musicians worried for years that if their song was covered successfully, it meant an erasure of their original. Padgett vehemently disagrees with that conclusion. For him, a cover expands the original, adds new textures and contexts, invites a new audience to enjoy the update and revisit the old. In other words, a successful cover makes the original stronger.

She made herself known that balmy January day of 2022 not through sight, or sound, but smell. Warm jambalaya and cold, olive-stuffed muffulettas waited upstairs at Schoen & Son Funeral Home on Canal Street in New Orleans, where my mother and I would eat after we'd said goodbye to Gloria.

Though I didn't speak at the memorial, I thought a lot about what I'd say. One of the things that made Gloria the best was that she was legitimately interested in what I thought, which stroked my ego in a way my busy mother couldn't always do. But she was also interested in everyone else too. There was some artistry, I suppose, in how she plumbed the depths of why people were the way they were. This is why she had so many conservative friends despite being one of the most politically liberal people I knew. Proof was all around me in the hundreds at the memorial, a great gathering of both the masked and unmasked.

The first to eulogize her was a young attorney, one of many for whom Gloria worked at the downtown law firm where she and my mother were legal secretaries for almost four decades. The attorney made a joke about the great unmasked, saying it was a testament to Gloria's patience and grace that there were so many Trump supporters in the room. It reminded me that when Trump first came down that godforsaken escalator, right around the time Gloria was diagnosed with breast cancer (proof that if there's a god, he's a bastard), I raged and scoffed at the stupidity of anyone who could consider this monstrous moron as anything but a joke. Gloria reminded me that listening to others' wrong-headed ideas strengthens our positions, because we're empathizing where they won't.

Over a dozen people spoke beautifully at the memorial, including members of the great unmasked, but it was her college-aged niece whose impromptu speech most touched me. "I didn't plan to say anything, but, my Aunt Gloria, there's probably no other person as responsible for making me who I am as she was. She shared with me what was good, what was cool. Every piece of music I listen to or television I watch and love is because of her. I can't imagine not being able to talk to her about any of it anymore."

But silence touched me as well. During the parade of memorial speakers, I asked my mother if she wanted to say something, said I'd hold her hand and walk up there with her, if she liked. She gently shook her head, and later, in the privacy of plating our jambalaya and muffulettas, said it'd been enough for her to tell Gloria's family everything she felt, what losing her meant—losing the best friend she'd ever had, losing a piece of herself. In Gloria's final days under home hospice care, Mom had been with her. She held her hand, watched her slowly go. She didn't need to enact or perform her love.

It's regrettable how much I learned about Gloria from her obituary and memorial, simple facts I'd never bothered asking her about. Like me, she attended Nicholls State in Thibodaux, Louisiana (a.k.a. Harvard on the Bayou) and graduated from LSU. How had we never discussed that, or how had I forgotten? She was born earlier than I'd thought, in 1958, the same year, in fact, that Andy Williams swiped inside his cheek in the chorus of The Chordettes' "Lollipop," the very first sound I conjured when my water broke. The song "Lollipop" itself is a cover, first recorded by a long-forgotten duo named Ronald & Ruby. The oddly, wonderfully comparable sound would've never entered my mind upon my daughter's arrival had it not been for The Chordettes and Andy Williams's famous *pop*.

Covers are so ubiquitous now that we take for granted the term itself—why they're called covers at all—and as stated in Padgett's *Cover Me*, there are three theories for its derivation. The first is that a music label would "cover its bets" by releasing a recording of a popular song; in the second, the idea was that the new version would literally "cover up" the old on record store shelves; and the third, most capitalistic theory was how music label execs would answer, when asked if they had any copycat versions of a popular song to release: "We've got it covered!"

I can't help but find a metaphor in these theories and how they apply to the relationships I've held most dearly. Having a child is a way to cover your bets: if you can't get everything you want out of this life, maybe your child can. Maybe they can cover up your shittiness, your aging, your (hopefully) slow bodily unraveling. If you choose to have children, a secret, sacred hope is that when you get old, they'll care for you; they'll have you covered.

Before deciding to have children, and still, I've been both afraid to be covered and afraid not to be. I've feared motherhood would mean half-measures in artistry and vice versa. And I've feared the obverse:

that without motherhood, I'd have no excuse, no cover, for any mediocre art. But in listening to "One" again to write this essay, perhaps more obsessively than I did twenty years ago, after rehearing the lament of being *one*, I see that although I planned to take Gloria's path and instead took my mother's, the two paths weren't discrete at all. The overlap lives in their love for each other. "One" can be sad, but "two" can be too, and children won't always cover our loneliness or any other parts of us that need covering. This essay is an inadequate cover for the originality, the oneness, of Gloria. And of Aimee Mann. And of being a mother to my daughter and a daughter to my mother. But I'm making this cover anyway. I'm still singing the song I've heard before, only singing it differently.

I've learned, too, that the concept of covers is relatively modern. Before the advent of rock 'n' roll, it was the song that was paramount, not the singer. The quality of the song mattered more than the person performing it. So to extend that cover-as-relationship metaphor, if my daughter is my cover, the question isn't what she makes of me or I of her; the singular song she makes of her life is what counts. My daughter, my cover, who first made herself known, truly, not through sight or sound or smell but touch. After twelve hours of labor, when she crowned, then blinked, then screamed, I brought her to my breast, and tasted what it was for me to be born into someone irrevocably different, both alone and not alone, not joined together anymore, but not two, either, and never quite *one* again.

AN ESSAY ENTITLED "MRS."

I

It is an essay told in three parts: the narrator's sister is the titular main character. It begins with the irony that though Mrs. is unmarried with five children from two different men, when she's happy and in love, she refers to herself as Mrs. Surname-of-whomever-she's-dating-at-the-time.

It details salient incidents of her Mrs.-dom: how her first Mr., suspicious of infidelity, once cracked her over and over with a leather whip; how he once threw her mother into a window, leaving a Pangea-shaped bruise; how he kidnapped Mrs., abandoning their toddlers screaming *mommy* back at the apartment while he pulled her by the ponytail into the car, stabbing her leg with a penknife, the hole in her pants blooming into a rose, then drove her away for hours, promising the end, before inexplicably bringing her back home.

Here we insert historical references as a respite from savagery: according to the OED, the first printed "Mrs." appears in 1485 London, where a Mres. Sucklyng bequeaths a "gyfte." The dictionary affirms the contemporary appropriateness of our Mrs.'s usage: the title now applies without discrimination.

At this point we note the traditional inheritance of our fathers' names, which, if we're females entering heteronormative marriage structures, we go on to reidentify through our husbands. Feminists, like the narrator, who don't take their husbands' names, thus represent their fathers' legacies. Even if their father, let's say, once whacked their mother's leg with a golf club when she laughed at his shanked putt.

The first section ends by returning to our Mrs.: how had she allowed this to happen?

II

The section in which the answer is made known. The narrator/main character's mother married three times, and all three husbands laid hands on her. The first phone number the narrator ever dialed was 9-1-1, the den a panopticon of flashing lights—*red fish, blue fish.*

The idiom "laying on of hands" is derived from dozens of biblical references, where, as in life, it cuts both ways. Jesus's famous hand healing in Luke and Mark and Acts. But then in 1 Timothy 5:22: "Lay hands suddenly on no [one]; keep thyself pure." Whether that purity pertains to averting envy or lust or wrath does not present itself in this context.

Where the question is asked: If epigenetics gets the idea of inherited trauma correctly, then is the abuse of Mrs. learned or is it biological legacy? A line of women's names lost to dust, to fathers and husbands, women who screamed out and ran scared and hit back and believed in redemption and revenge and felt free and felt loved but were also beaten down, by hands and spit and whips and words. Whatever was available, these gyftes to and from our mothers.

III

In the final section, past is prologue. Here the narrator returns to her university's library archives, to a 1895 journal from Blocton, Alabama, penned by a woman referring to herself as *Mrs.* Narrative evidence of her husband's years of abuse. The parasol he gifted, then broke over her head. Her packed trunk hidden under the bed. Names of witnesses who'd testify, their addresses. This journal, palm sized, pored over and caressed like a talisman.

Where the narrator reveals her use of third person as obfuscation: that she has feigned ethnographer when she's the autobiographer.

An Essay Entitled "Mrs."   133

Her own journals, written many years ago but throbbingly alive, reveal similar stories. How she knows precisely what it feels like to have hands lain, wrapped around her neck. Mouth hooked like a fish to pull her up to meet him or dragged down to the floor where it belonged. In the journals, in the past.

In the present, her daughter is the gift. When caressing her head at night, the narrator wishes to make a permanent helmet of her hands, for her hands to transmute the power to rescind legacy. The narrator, remember, is me, the legacy mine to give. But since there's no permanence in a mother's hands, in the future, when my daughter uses her grown hands to trace the lines my former lover gifted me, I long for this: should she meet some version of him, in a classroom, in a bar, she'll find something so recognizable, so uninteresting in his demonic smile, she won't be tempted to learn how that story will end. Here in my hands, through the sheer naming of myself, I carry the hope that my daughter, and hers and hers and hers, might be bequeathed a different gift: a different kind of name.

HOW NOT TO
HATE YOUR WRITING

First, try to hate something, anything, else. One of your sisters perhaps, her incessant kid-stagramming, which when contrasted with your current childlessness and paltry essaying, shows without telling what creation *really* looks like.

Or hate the earnest grocery cashier who asks during your nightly Yellow Tail pinot noir purchase if she can see your identification. Not your ID: your *identification*. Who doesn't smile back when you joke that she's probably memorized your height, weight, and address by now. Who makes you wonder if you can't *say* anything right, how you are ever going to *write* anything right.

Run the two of them off a cliff together, Thelma-and-Louise style, in your essay in search of a beginning. Hate them with every clip of your typing fingertips. Hate them with the scorching of a thousand venereal diseases.

Once you're piping hot, level out your hatred. Hate them merely with the scorching of a handful of venereal diseases.

Understand time's power to stale. See your writing as a slice of Bunny Bread, a brand you crave the day you purchase it, though in a few days you'll see how briefly viable is even the bunniest of bread. Next month you'll forget the brand you craved, and in six the loaf will be unrecognizable. It would be better used as a doorstopper, like the draft of the great American novel you will never write.

So, butter your writing with care. Wait till the butter is a little soft and the bread a little toasted so that it will spread easily. Time is the butter. Your desire to not hate your own writing is your mouth, chewing.

Acknowledge bad metaphors. Tell yourself that staying hungry is among the most important of the bad ones, because it's true. If a mentor advises this, don't think back to the Bunny Bread. Eat the double chocolate cupcake or whatever you're craving and for those few nanoseconds the bad metaphors will disappear.

Your sister will not want to read your work or your father won't. This will help. You'll know that before you even ask them to, because a writing professor will have warned you by saying, "The world isn't asking to read your work; indeed, it may often ask whether or not it needs more writers."

Acknowledge this deep truth. Think the sentence, "Oh well; only dicks speak in semicolons."

Write the sentence, "My writing professor, while correct, has the charm of so many buttholes."

Write a sentence that includes the oft-used poetry phrase "like so many" and then vow to never write those three words in succession ever again.

Sing a few of your worst lines to the beat of Beyonce's "Halo." Or Peter Cetera's "The Glory of Love." YouTube the videos for both if, in addition to avoiding hating your writing, you'd like to understand less about what it means to sing—or write—about love.

Write a shallow imitation of one of your favorite writers. Do not acknowledge this anywhere in your piece and see if readers will notice. Include your favorite writer's name as a header and then erase it. Next, type your own name in the most professional font and size, print it, and paste it to the copy of your favorite book by your favorite writer. These two unrelated activities will be so exhausting that now you will be too tired to hate your own writing.

Log on to your favorite social networking site and note writing that is so much easier to hate than your own. See your writer friends posting witty, quippish updates? They are trying really hard to do that and want your approval. Honor the most desperate one with a Like, but give big Loves to nonwriter high school friends who post sentences like, "Ges what immmmm doingggggg?!!!"

Read the Drudge Report, listen to Alex Jones. Hate that hateful shit instead.

Jot down your next story idea longhand, but use your opposing hand, preferably after ingesting the bottle of wine for which grocery store *identification* was required. This text cannot be hated because it will be incomprehensible. Thus, erudite. Thus, you are brilliant.

Suspect your writing of having an affair with your best writer friend. Leave your friend a vague message: *I know what you're trying to do to us*, and then silence your phone.

Win your writing back. Print out every page you've written in the past six months and line your bed with it. Light some sexy candles. Or sexily light some regular candles. Whatever. See what happens.

Try not to hate anything or anyone too much, or risk becoming a major bitch and an unsuccessful writer. (Ideally, in your quest to not hate your writing, you want those last two adjectives reversed.)

BOBBITT

For as long as I can remember, I've believed that if there's such a thing as unequivocal truth in memory, it's this: decades ago, when Univision first reported that years of physical and sexual abuse culminated one night in Lorena Bobbitt cutting off her husband's penis, my grandmother, Lala, plucked a banana from the ceramic fruit bowl, pointed to my grandfather and said, "Never fuck with an Ecuadorian woman, *hijo de puta*." If my adolescence has an origin story, it's this one, how I defined myself against her. Be smaller, quieter, beware the power and danger of becoming this kind of woman, despite growing at turns ashamed of and downright obsessed with these kinds of women and their powers.

But there isn't, and it doesn't, because the scene couldn't have happened this way. My grandfather, Abuelo, died in 1990, and John Bobbitt was de-Bobbitted in 1993.

My favorite Lala legend, once I reached an age where I esteemed rather than dreaded her stories, is the one with the hot pepper. Abuelo, a serial cheater, had abandoned his family for six months to live with another woman and then suddenly came home one evening, begging forgiveness. He'd missed them too much, he'd said, *te estraño*— same line he'd used after previous affairs. This time Lala accepted his apology. She served him dinner. She forced their kids to hug him; my mother remembers the smell of Paco Rabanne pressed into her unwilling face. After weeks of banishment Lala finally allowed his reentry to their bedroom. That first night back in their bed together, Abuelo slid under their Downy-dried sheets, penance complete, home at last. He curled over onto his routine right side, his back to her. She quietly retrieved surgical gloves from her nightstand drawer and slipped them on, then unwrapped an Ecuador Hot—185,000 on the Scoville Heat Unit scale—from a plastic baggie. She spooned him from behind, tucked her arm under the back of his drawstring pajama pants as if to make an amorous move. And then, she stuffed it inside him.

Thus, the story ingrained in all the women in our family, and the men we married, was not that Abuelo abandoned Lala for another woman, that Lala sought factory shift work to make ends meet, that she was cuckqueaned and made to feel low many times over. Oh, no. She was the anal pepper stuffer. The no-shit-taker, the not-to-be-fucked-with. We Robles women show our gratitude for this legacy in how we retell and perform our Lala stories. If I were telling this one aloud right now, I'd poke my right pointer finger into my left fist to demonstrate.

Decades later, I wonder if Bobbitt—as name, as symbol—is more synonymous with the person being castrated or the one doing the castrating? *Lorena*, a 2019 documentary produced by Jordan Peele that attempts to do for gender justice what the *O.J.: Made in America* doc did for racial justice, proposes that the true, untold story about the Bobbitts is not what she did to him, but what he did to her all those nights and years before the incident. She is most accurately defined not as the woman who did *it*, but who many times was *done-to*.

But both aspects of Lorena are essential to understand the context of what happened that night, because humans are complicated. Pure victims and villains reside in popcorn movies, not in our real lives. Still, in my mind, Lorena was always most compelling as the actor. And depending on your perspective, the actor was the villain.

Of our family's orally anthologized Lala stories, one of my mother's most cherished is called Palm Sunday. Once, in the late 1960s, during my mother's own adolescence, Lala suspected Abuelo of cheating again. So she did something I still find inconceivable after a lifetime of hearing this tale. When he announced that Sunday morning that he would go to church alone, Lala hid in the trunk of his Buick. Then he parked and left the car for the service, and she slipped out of the trunk, hiding in the backseat for an hour to see if he came out alone. After the bells chimed and the church doors opened to release the holy masses, she peeked up and saw his balding head, *el cabrón*, and that he was holding hands with a brunette. The woman's hair was woven into a fashionable beehive, and Lala watched him lead her toward his car, each of them holding their sacred palms. Lala slunk out onto the driver's side and hunched next to its tires, still unsure of her next move. Abuelo gallantly opened the passenger door for his guest, tossing both large palms in the backseat where Lala had lain seconds before. That's when Lala pulled out the palms still smelling of Chrism oil, intended to emanate the "odor of sanctity," ran over to the passenger side and began smacking them both, unspooling the woman's beehive around her wrists, while the Latinas leaning over wrought-iron balconies on Elysian Fields Boulevard egged her on. *Dale, dale, mujer, buen hecho!* After their fifteen-minute drive back home to Michoud Boulevard, Lala was still palm smacking him, *andate a la mierda, hijo de su madre.* How scary my mother remembered it being back then. How funny now. Both versions and tones true.

There's a quieter story I didn't share at the memorial a couple of years ago when Lala died. When she first entered Wynhoven Healthcare Center in New Orleans's Westbank and correctly predicted this would be her final home on this Earth, she made an announcement. *Tengo un secreto. But it's something I can't tell you till I'm closer to death. So you'll remember me better.*

Dígame ahorita! I pleaded. *You'll forget.* Like many of my people, I covet secrets, and once granted access must dispense them widely, my heart bursting. But we both forgot. I became preoccupied with the birth of my daughter, and in those last years, Lala poked her memory's embers in solitude. She died and left no evidence of this last story she meant to tell. Her *gran secreto* is now whatever I decide it is, using the shards of every tale she's told me, and the ones we experienced together, to piece it out.

After Lala's memorial, my aunt-by-marriage, long divorced from my Uncle Carlos, demurred during the exultant Lala stories, picked nervously at her black lace dress as she lamented the shame of Abuelo abusing Lala. This history of violence, Carlos had told her long ago, was why he'd always had a problem with his temper, and why, in turn, he routinely abused my aunt, even hurt their toddler daughter, whom he'd once flung into the wall like a rag doll. It was a tidy-bow narrative my aunt told herself to explain their toxic relationship. Abuelo hit his wife, and in turn his son hit her.

Could *that* have been Lala's secret? It doesn't comport with how I saw either her or Abuelo while they were alive. In my memory all five feet of her tower over his nearly six feet, because in my memory he always sits, cornered in his La-Z-Boy while she shouts down, arms everywhere, and because memory trumps anatomy and physiology. Lala was also psychologically cruel to him. She frequently called him *"hijo de cura,"* son of a priest, which I believed for years was a term of endearment. I'm not sure when I finally did the math on that one— that being related to a holy man could only come to fruition through unholy means. In this case, Abuelo's not-so-much-a-secret is that in the late nineteenth century, when a British priest came to Guayaquil to convert the heathens, he unintentionally converted Abuelo's grandmother into her pregnancy. So Lala's derision was slightly off; technically, Abuelo was the grandson of a priest.

Of all Lala's feasible secrets—she'd always loved another man (or woman!); she'd had her own desperate, loveless affair; she harbored some grand ambition unfulfilled—could she have been just another sufferer at the hands of her man? But wasn't what was so plainly true about her the opposite, that she was not the victim who was done unto, but the actor, the doer, my villain?

Lorena, both then and now, remembers certain consequential details from the night of June 23, 1993, and totally blanks on others. According to court testimony, she claimed her husband came home drunk and raped her yet again. Once he passed out, she fled to the kitchen, filled with fear and rage and no person with whom to vent it, no common language with which to express it. Twenty-six years later, blonde and in her late forties, Lorena remembers pictures in her mind. His insults, tearing at her underwear, countless anal rapes, threats to always find her no matter where she tries to escape. His chiseled face. Ice blue eyes. She remembers seeing the knife illuminated by the light from the refrigerator door but doesn't remember concluding she needed to use it. She doesn't remember slicing.

This section of the documentary is hard to watch. She's clearly still in pain after all this time, uncomfortable telling this part of the story. Sitting next to me, my husband is also uncomfortable hearing it.

"I mean, he's a monster, of course. But it's that . . ." He doesn't seem to know what to say next. "But she cut his dick off."

"Oh, I know," I say.

"Imagine the reality of doing it. I mean, you'd have to be an insane person."

"Uh huh," I say. Because of who I come from, "insane person" or its sister term, "crazy woman," are not pejoratives but low-key badges of honor. I don't tell him that, though, but munch my popcorn as the saga I thought I already knew continues unfurling onscreen.

During the 1994 trial against Lorena, the world debated the validity of her recollections. Though we know much more now about how common faulty memories are in abuse victims, both for psychological and physiological reasons (repeated blows to the head during any given moment, for instance, will weaken its memories), this was the main thrust of the prosecution's case back then. What she remembered and what she didn't was convenient to her defense; thus, she was a liar. Not to mention she was an Ecuadorian immigrant, a foreigner, which at certain times in this country can feel like a crime in itself.

Arguments against her, both from media figures and zealous passersby interviewed on the streets, devolved from there. She desperately needed a green card. She possessed a jealous, frightful temper. She wanted only to keep her husband's lovely penis from other women. Cumulatively, these are interesting arguments to make about her because, on the one hand, she's an inherently violent, emotionally volatile Latina, but, on the other, she's cold and calculating, in total control of her actions. She knew what she would do with that knife. But these debates work under narrow conditions because, when Lorena herself projected simultaneous strength and weakness, she was accused of disingenuousness. Juror Kenneth Hulse bemoaned her various self-presentations, performing that age-old deconstruction of a woman's personality based on her sartorial choices. Why, he wondered aloud, did she sometimes wear simple dresses (a frail victim's clothes, he seems to say) and other days wear bolder outfits with done-up hair and makeup (hellfire villain, clearly). For him, one of these bifurcated identities had to be a lie. Pick a single way to be, he seemed to imply—stop confusing us with your complications.

Lala, too, was multifaceted, which makes any attempt to render a clear description of her, much less decipher her *gran secreto*, impossible. She was temptress in one moment, chaste maiden in another. When I was a teenager, during and after the Lorena years, she developed the regrettable habit of grabbing my friends' breasts and genitals. My best girlfriend Danielle would come over, and Lala would tightly embrace her, bouncing her up and down, saying, *oy mijita, que grande, lemme check how big*, and squeeze the sides of her breasts. Danielle would giggle uncomfortably, and I'd dive onto my bed and scream into my pillow. My neighbor Jim, a year older than me, often mowed our lawn, and once, Lala peeked through the blinds at him and said, *I wonder if his banana is ripe yet. Tienes hambre?* She wanted to know, disgustingly, if her observation made me hungry. "Gross!" I said, "Shut up!" When he came inside, asking for a glass of water, she widened her eyes, mouth agape.

"*Brooksita*, I can't believe you said that."

I knew her games but was powerless to stop them.

"What?" said Jim, all freckled innocence, wiping the sweat from his eyes with the collar of his shirt.

"Brooksita said she was *curiosa* about your banana size. Then she said she was *hungry*."

"*Maldita mentirosa!*" I screamed, calling her a damned liar before storming off to my room. I knew full well my hysterics made me look even guiltier of this banana talk but so what. Anyone who believed Lala was an asshole. Even though, despite knowing better, that asshole was often me.

This was the Lala of my adolescence. And yet she could be so chained to propriety. Several years after this rhetorical and physical obsession with pubescent private parts, once my stepsister Alley became a teenager, I returned home from graduate school in Baton Rouge to visit my family in New Orleans. Lala grabbed both of my hands and led me to my old bedroom. She had something scandalous to tell me, but I had to keep it a secret.

"*Mi corazón, ay Dios mío, es terible*, you won't believe it."

Uh huh.

Then she proceeded, in graphic detail, to describe how she'd caught Alley and her boyfriend making out in our living room, on the kitchen stools, on the floor next to the dining room table, hands everywhere, oh the noise, how she moaned, how they moved! Completely without irony, Lala performed the gestures and the moaning, gyrating her hips and assaulting the air to show how horrific they were, as she repeated, *Terible!* She seemed to thoroughly enjoy recounting this *experencia* that had nearly given her a heart attack.

"Lala," I said, ready with a defense's eye for logic. "This didn't happen. Alley lives across town, in Chalmette, with her mother. If she would sneak in to hook up while everyone was gone, why would she do it while you were here?"

"I was in the bathroom. I'll bet she thought the house was empty!"

"With your Toyota out front?"

"I saw what I saw!"

"Is there a chance you were imagining things? Daydreaming?"

"*Mi Dios* would never allow me a dream *tan espantoso*."

Our polemic continued from there until she threw up her arms (*aye, qué pesada!*) and fled to the kitchen to pout. I couldn't understand how this teller of illustrious vengeances, this purveyor of bawdy talk, could so fiercely demur at another's imagined amorousness. It's like she needed any lustiness to be her idea, to be the center of whatever mood she decided to create. She was an actor, for good or for ill.

Only in hindsight do I see these identities—rakish liar, girlish inno-cent—as not bifurcated at all. The girlishness was always a part of the rake, and vice versa. Sincere desires underpinned: to be looked at and heard, understood and misunderstood, thought about and dissected. In her own small ways, within the family who feared and adored her, she needed to wield power.

Though the term was not a part of our lexicon the night of the slice felt round the world, in the early 1990s, memory researchers were nearly two decades into studying the phenomenon of "flashbulb events." The term is defined as an autobiographical memory, fully il-luminated and detailed, being captured in one moment, that also tran-spires during an historic, cultural event. Where you were on 9/11, for instance, or when the *Challenger* exploded. Or when you heard Lo-rena slashed. Time slice errors, a related term, develop when a cou-ple of events happen in the same general timeframe as a major media event, and we get the sequence jumbled up. Under these circum-stances, memory is more fungible than ever.

Flashbulb memories and time slice errors apply here because since Lala's funeral, since her death and my attempts to excavate her *se-creto*, I'm remembering her differently—and myself with her. How the last few times I asked Lala to tell me the one with the hot pep-per, she wasn't as happy to tell it as I was to hear it (*ay, déjame en paz*, she'd say, *enough with that*). How I always poke my finger in my hand to demonstrate the story because, though I adored Abuelo as my grandfather, I thought his pain as a husband was richly deserved. How as an adolescent I followed the Lorena trial closely, lingered on her wide-eyed sweetness, those lace-collar dresses, her doleful, down-turned eyes looking like a younger Lala who'd been rejected, and thought her so lovely—but how mostly, I wanted to know what it felt like. To do the unimaginable. How in more recent memories of Lala's *jaja* on Bobbitt day, when I speak to my mom and sisters about them, I'm the one laughing maniacally, and how I remember an important detail now. I see myself in the living room mirror, the one with an embossed palm tree decal. Is it possible that the *hijo de puta* and banana pluck and flip were not Lala's moves, but mine?

As the heat of the trial against Lorena Bobbitt was dying down in the summer of 1994, I met my first real boyfriend. In January, Lorena had been acquitted of assault on her husband and sent to a mandatory forty-five days of therapy in a psychiatric ward. Is it valid to grant any seriousness to my childhood relationship from twenty-five years ago? Young love. First love. In the documentary, that's how both John and Lorena described their meeting, when she was nineteen, and he was two years older. They held hands, chastely sipping from the same milkshake across a table at the local DQ.

The "young" part is where the similarities end between my first relationship and theirs, because he and I were volatile from the outset. It began with playful, flirtatious pushing and slapping, a reason to touch. But the first time he slapped my face hard, I tackled him, stretched his Duck Head collar and punched his chest awkwardly. He flipped me over and held me down on my wisteria-patterned bedspread, arms pinned over my head, and let a long, slow trail of spittle plop onto my face. We stayed frozen like that for several seconds before he let me up, long enough for me to accept what had happened. I was now the spit-upon. "Don't fight with me, I'll always win," he said, laughing. Because this was all a joke, not a real fight. We were kids. But I sensed I'd lost something, and I wanted to win. To be on top, him begging me to stop, using the power of my teeth or saliva or the butts from my head. This moment, wiping his saliva from my cheek, was my first anticipation of vengeance. This was the beginning of our courtship.

Which continued with me, intermittently, getting my ass whooped. I use that expression to deflect its dirtier facts. A punch in the back, over and over in the same spot, with two protruding knuckles for maximum efficacy; a grip on the neck to put me in my place, wherever he decided that was; my feet swiped and pushed from behind so I'd fall on my face . . . some of it play, all of it real, never understanding the line from one realm to the other. Me, Lala's granddaughter, a victim? Impossible. I fought back; I was a no-shit taker! But receiving and causing hurt was a secret I hid beneath toughness and the ability to laugh through pain with the ease of Lala. Nothing could hurt if everything was a joke. This lie was a secret that for so long I kept even from myself.

Just once in my memory of this relationship did I get my chance to win. I can't remember what instigated it (many of our fights were, absurdly, about one of us having a normal conversation with a member of the opposite sex), but I do remember feeling when I landed a decisive punch that this was about something bigger: every time he hurt me. That's for that hand to the neck, motherfucker! That's for the headbutt that had me seeing white. There was glory in every blow. I remember wondering if that was how it felt to hurt me. True invincibility. And the best part was, he couldn't hit back—he was so drunk, having shown up at my house from a party he'd forbidden me from attending, he could barely roll over to deflect my assaults. For my part, I still don't know if I was enacting the sins of Lala or Abuelo, or of Lorena or John, by hurting him, and getting hurt by him. If all of this was performativity that I'd learned not only from how he treated me but from Lala and her stories. Had I sought out someone who I'd want vengeance against, who'd give me the chance to fight, because that's what our women do? Back in that moment, I remember stepping on his hand and slowly applying pressure, watching him struggle to be released. His chiseled face. Hazel eyes. I don't remember the days or weeks after, or the next time we kissed.

It occurs to me now how much my mother is implicated in this legacy too. While my first love and I somehow managed to keep our fights a secret inside my bedroom, my mother fought with her husband out in the open, intermittently, usually on whiskey-fueled nights. The Lorena connections are strong in her too. My mom looks a lot like Lorena, and she married a man with certain Bobbitt characteristics, the kind of guy who would decal his truck with a giant spider sticker that matches his forearm tattoo. John Bobbitt, along with being a serial batterer, is the dude who, after having his penis severed and reattached—the first surgery of this kind in history—would go on to star in a couple of porno flicks, one in which a Lorena look-alike (but with gargantuan breasts) ravenously seduces him in order to maim him, and another called *Frankenpenis*, whose plot I guess is self-explanatory. For a legacy of no-shit-takers, we Ecuadorian women sure eat a lot of it.

One part of the *Lorena* documentary gives me pause. Early on in the series, John Bobbitt's defense attorney, Gregg Murphy, claims John wasn't the violent one in the relationship. It was Lorena. Even now he maintains this assertion. Police records reveal that once, while Lorena was still married to John, her own mother, Elvia Gallo, called 9-1-1 on her daughter for assaulting him. This incident is later abandoned as a thread in the narrative. The documentary also leaves out Lorena's subsequent 1997 assault charge from her mother; Lorena purportedly punched Elvia while the two were watching television, though Lorena was later acquitted. What's the explanation for these episodes? In the earlier one, was it possible that Elvia tried to save Lorena from John's violence, called the cops before it could escalate, and blamed her daughter for fear of John's retaliation? Or did the two women also have a harmful tit-for-tat relationship? Or, did Lorena strike out, seemingly unprovoked? Though we may never know, though Lorena herself might not even remember, my guess is Lorena did strike out. Because violence begets violence. Because people teach each other how to treat each other. Because maybe when she got the chance to retaliate, Lorena got her licks in. Whatever the case, I wish it were explored more in *Lorena*, or in our public consciousness, because for me Lorena's potential acts of violence don't detract from her story—they amplify it. She didn't deserve a second of the violence she got. But she didn't necessarily roll over and take every second of it either. It's the latter that makes me love her.

The writer, like the documentarian, constructs, repackages, misjudges, and concludes, in the midst of fleeting action, no matter how powerful or terrifying, whatever gets pushed in or sliced off in any discrete moment in human history. Whatever her memories' flaws, she sets the permanent record. This is Lorena's role in the documentary. Though John and Lorena are both interviewed, she gets the lion's share of time and sympathy. It's called *Lorena*, after all, not *Bobbitt*. It's her story. Like it's Lala's. And my mother's. And mine.

Two of the writer's greatest gifts are quiet and control, qualities Lala and I—and some would say Latinas—lack. In retrospect, the catalyst of my own rage in relationships, that first one, especially, has been a lack of language control; I've had an inability to express the narrative of why I felt the way I felt in any given moment, especially those most contentious ones. Lorena had trouble communicating with her husband, as she was still relatively new to the English language. By contrast, Lala and I shared the same language as the men who harmed us and who we harmed. But could we say precisely in what ways they made us feel beholden or small or unseen or hurt? Rather than try to explain, sometimes it's easier to shout, to stuff, to swing.

The documentary concludes with an empowering narrative of how Lorena has gone on to create the Lorena Gallo Foundation, a program that supports victims of domestic violence, and I admire her doing so. Never again will I be a victim, she seems to say. And yet . . . the name feels off. Because while I loathe the tradition of women subjugating themselves to their husbands by taking their surnames to begin with, when I think of "Bobbitt," I don't think of John at all—that average name, that below-average man. Bobbitt is Lorena. Bobbitt is the women in my family. Because Lorena didn't just take his name in the matrimonial way, she confiscated it. Bobbitt has become a verb. It's become a deconstruction. It's become what a woman can do to you, if you fuck with her. *Hijo de puta, I'll Bobbitt you*, Lala might've said, or I might have. Bobbitt is an acceptance of the narrative that we went through something we're not proud of, a time when lines were so blurred it became difficult to see the difference between our villainy and victimhood, but it's something no man or boy gave to us. It's ours. We took it.

Lorena told her side of the story in the documentary in order to, as she says, set the record straight. I'm telling these stories to resurrect the palm leaf, to comb both large and small details of Lala's life to uncover the secret she promised, or invented, or to discover the secret of my own self. To see more clearly in the mirror. The narrative isn't tidy—there's no bow at its conclusion. No magical secret will be revealed. There's just a pepper and some palm smacks and our memories and their flaws. I'm trying to answer the question, how much of Lala is ingrained in me, and where do I resist her Bobbittry? In telling her stories, even after a lifetime of doing so, I'm only beginning to uproot some answers. Though there are no clear resolutions, unlike Lala, I won't wait till my deathbed to take a stab at them. These lines are my surgical gloves, these are our secrets. Remember us now.

THE CASE FOR "CUNT"

I haven't always known exactly what a *cock-sucking motherfucker* was, or why my father knew so many of them. But from the time I was still feeding from my mother's tit, I heard my father's *tits*, *shit*, *asshole*, and *fuck* more frequently than "I love you." Though to be fair, cursing is like a love language in New Orleans. *Son of a bitch* is merely the sound of coming home. Not everyone raised in the city talks this way, but few would look at you sideways if you did.

As an adult, I look at someone sideways when, after talking for some time, I realize they haven't used a single curse. *What in the ever-loving fuck is wrong with you?* I want to ask. Yet because I'm Latina, I've also learned to carefully calibrate my swearing, especially among those I don't know well. I can't drop a "cunt" on an English department colleague after we've finished chatting about the weather, for example. Even if I've scrolled through Twitter, and a "cunt" is sorely needed. I live in the Deep South and am aware that the language that comes most naturally to me is generally considered deplorable or un-academic or less generously the work of the devil. So I love my swearing, and my swearing is a constant worry.

Because my father worked as a ship's steward in the years before Hurricane Katrina, where his all-male shipmates spent lots of time imagining aloud the elaborate uses for ends of mop handles, and because he's a man, the thought of apologizing for his language has never crossed his mind. My whole life he's abused the English language in the most glorious ways. *Goddamn evil Republican sons of bitches.*

(Republican-led Congress voted on a tax break for the wealthy and balked on economic aid for the poor and middle classes.) *Fat sonofabitching fuck, go eat your damn pancakes.* (Chris Christie on *Meet the Press*.) *Get off the stage, you Willie Nelson–looking cunty bastard.* (This one was for Madonna, for daring to perform into her sixties, no longer as young and beautiful as she once was.) All of these responses reveal an irascible old man at his linguistic worst. But he doesn't really mean the meanness so much as he needs to say the curse.

I hate my father's language for its misogyny, its political effrontery, its callousness for humanity. Yet I love it because, despite myself, dammit, he makes me laugh. He once told me that if his doctor ever advised him to quit drinking for good, "I'd kill myself dead right inside the dickhead's office." My father's father died of cirrhosis in his fifties, and while wasting away in the hospital, he begged for liquor to be transmitted through an IV, and the story goes that someone snuck in a flask now and again to help calm him.

My father claims to never feel sad or existentially low; he calls me and curses about real and imagined infractions by a wide range of bastards, regarding people either televised or in the flesh. Research cited in Katherine Dunn's *On Cussing* confirms swearing helps us deal with pain. Though her example refers to physical suffering—studies show people who immerse their hands in ice water can endure it longer if they curse aloud—I believe this applies to emotional distress too. My father's stories and the curses that comprise them—negotiating with cocksuckers, most often—are all the therapy he needs.

For most of my life it's been "like father, like daughter" in the language arena, but for a while I've felt I should curb my enthusiasm for swearing. For one, my daughter attends an Episcopal preschool where they expect some propriety. One morning a couple years ago, her teacher approached my passenger window to chitchat while I waited in the pick-up line. I asked how she'd behaved that day because, "Her sleep last night was for shit." The teacher's face crumpled like looseleaf paper, and she responded more to the car door than me. "You sure do put it out there! You don't mince words!" I mean, she's right,

I don't, but I didn't see anything particularly off-color about what I'd said. What's a quiet little "shit" between two adults?

"Oh. Haha," I said. "So, was she okay?" The teacher said that my daughter had performed her routine number of breakdowns. My next few sentences emerged, linguistically, in the vein of Mary Poppins. "How terribly unfortunate! She behaves abominably when she sleeps poorly." People who balk at my natural inclination for expression make me quite literally unlike myself. I regretted that "shit" slip for weeks. I can't imagine what the teacher would think about my ration of "cunts" per day, particularly during an election season.

Which is a forever-season in twenty-four-hour-news-cycle American politics, and which reminds me that our most recent ex-president bragged on tape about how much he enjoys grabbing women by the pussy. Because, if you recall, they let him do it. Yet he was elected in spite of (because of?) this revelation. More than 70 percent of American evangelicals let him do it, too, since they voted him into office, and, even at the end of the most deranged, debased presidency in modern history, a majority of them still supported him. I understand they're experiencing cognitive dissonance, they believe he's an imperfect conduit of God, etc., etc., but you have to lean on that magical thinking pretty hard with this particular asshole.

But I have another theory about why they allowed themselves to ignore the "pussy" talk. According to Melissa Mohr's *Holy Shit: A Brief History of Swearing*, curse words can historically be divided into two main areas of taboo: the Holy (religion-oriented curses) and the Shit (swears involving the human body). Yet in the past few decades, a new taboo swear category emerged in the racial epithet. My guess is that even though the religious right dislikes the ex-president's vulgarity, they can abide shit/body-type curses, even those rife with misogyny, that have become generally less taboo across culture. However, if he were known to have used a racial slur that has become increasingly off limits, even Senator Mitch McConnell might not allow the president to grab him by the pussy.

This begs the question of which we'd consider worse—the former president's long history of blatant racism in the form of housing discrimination, the call for execution of the Central Park Five, the demand for the birth certificate of the first Black U.S. president, the brown children his administration locked in cages at our country's border with Mexico, on and fucking on—or, if we could find a short-hand moment of him speaking a single slur that would finally "prove" his racism. In our culture, despite what we believe about ourselves, despite what we purport to teach our children, words speak louder than actions.

Surely recordings of Trump's racial epithets exist. Right? Insiders say he swears more frequently than those around him, limited vocabulary that he has. One story from Michael Wolff's book on his presidency, *Siege*, recounts a rumor that somewhere in fourteen years of behind-the-scenes *Apprentice* footage, one contestant says the word "cunt," and another admonishes him that it's prohibited from television. To which the big D responds by saying the word four times in succession, proud, it seems from his tenor and mien, to establish himself as the Rosa Parks of "cunt."

I wonder what the public response would be if a woman running for higher office was rumored to ever have spoken the word "cunt." In the 1990s, Hillary Clinton said "cookies" in a context that many found insulting to the *real* women of America and has been castigated for it ever since.

Anyway, add this man's legacy, language, and lunacy to the reasons why I'm giving up on the curse. Or trying to.

Because while it's okay for me to occasionally "shit" on my daughter's teacher, if the teacher's okay with it, it's not okay for my daughter to do so. Several years ago, before my daughter was born, my husband and I visited my then-two-year-old niece in Baltimore. She was experimenting with talking and wanted to tell us about a character in her favorite cartoon, some mouse who sounded like a dick.

"He's not nice," she told us. "He's so . . . fucking."

"He's so what?" asked my husband, making sure he'd heard her right.

"He's so fucking!"

"He's so what?"

This back-and-forth continued a few more times, both because we were trying to parse her sentence construction, waiting for the "fucking" modifier to follow with a noun, but also because cursing toddlers are hilarious. The exception is when the toddler is your own. Because in that case, you're complicit in raising a feral child. Who wants to deal with the fallout of a kid who says to their teacher, "I don't want to play outside, fucker, I want to draw!"

Hearing my niece curse reminded me of an apocryphal story my mother loves telling about linguistically innocent kindergarten me. One day I returned from school in hysterics because a boy on the bus called me a name. No, I could not repeat the word, it was too terrible; I admitted it was "the j-word." My mother ticked down the list of possibilities. Did he call me a jerk? A jagoff? A . . . jackass?

"The last one, that's it!" I said, weeping into her arms.

But my mother wouldn't let it go there. "Did you say something that made him upset? Why did he call you that?"

"No reason!" I insisted. "I only called him 'motherfucker.'"

My mother stifled a laugh and explained that this was one of the worst "bad" words. "You should never say that at school, or ever, really."

"Then why do you?" I said, flatly.

It's a cute enough story. Again, any curse from a child's mouth is inherently funny since they can't yet comprehend its implications. It's the provenance of my own cursing life, that it all started with that harmless little "motherfucker."

But the more I've thought about it, the more cloying and untrue the story seems. Not that my mother is lying. I just can't understand in what context I'd call someone a "motherfucker," a word I'd heard her use in annoyance or anger, and expect anything other than an offended response. Clearly he'd pissed me off, so I called him a word matching that feeling. Did my child's mind read his "jackass" response, one I probably hadn't heard used much due to its candy-assed nature, as the real dialectical dagger, since it was unfamiliar? Did the utility I'd witnessed in both my parents' "motherfuckers" make them benign? My father spat it out constantly while traversing New Orleans traffic when he picked me up for the weekend, and it seemed to relieve his anger. I knew if he was calling someone else a motherfucker, he wouldn't be yelling at me.

A few semesters ago I taught a creative writing course on immersion, where my students' semester project was to ensconce themselves in an unfamiliar subculture for thirty days. An avowed atheist attended Catholic masses. A wallflower partied every weekend. A self-described Mac Daddy tried like hell to remain celibate for the month.

As for me, I quit cursing. I took on this project while six months pregnant, when I most wanted a salty margarita and to excoriate any shithead who undershot my due date. But I saw this constraint as ethos building. I'd adapt alongside my students and rid myself of this habit. I'd been swearing even more lately but had become particularly liberal with "cunt."

The day before I introduced this assignment, I'd returned home from the grocery and vented to my husband about that always-hellacious chore. "I got into the wrong line, of course. The cunt in front of me had a million coupons," I told him.

"Cunt, really?" he asked. My husband has no problem with my use of the word, but he reminded me that earlier that morning I'd also called our internet router a cunt. And my toe, when I stubbed it. I was constantly whispering in the presence of my toddler, thereby minimizing the point of the curse to begin with, which is to say it with gusto. It was time to abstain.

The young women in my immersion class loved that I was pregnant and that I cursed. A couple of them said I shouldn't stop. One who didn't, a Southern Belle who wore full pancake makeup at 9 a.m., offered "the kitchen lexicon" to help me curb cursing. "My gramma taught us to use food words," she said. "Say 'aw, sugar,' instead of the vulgar s-word. Or 'buttered toast.' Or 'son of a biscuit'!"

I might be a serial swearer, but I'm no savage. I respect my students. I didn't say aloud, "I would never fucking say any of those dumbass words." Instead, I suggested, "If we're going to use substitute amelioration for curses, we can do funnier than that."

"Why does being funny matter?" she asked. "And anyway, you can be funny without cursing." How to explain the wrongheadedness of her question and assertion? This lesson could take all semester.

≫⟩ ⟨≪

Decades ago when I was in college, I prided myself on being a guy's girl. Mine was a *fuck you, you fucking fuck* ethos that made me comfortable in a roomful of men. Because, as a Tau Kappa Epsilon once told me, "You're so dude-like, I don't even ever imagine having sex with you."

"You mean raping me," I countered. "No woman would willingly fuck you."

"See, that's what I'm talking about!" he said. "You're funny, like a guy!"

This dudebro likely hadn't heard of author Christopher Hitchens, but they espoused the same ideas. In 2007, Hitchens argued the reasons "Why Women Aren't Funny" in *Vanity Fair*. Obviously satirical yet still obnoxious, the essay argued that men's superior comedic skills were essential to the propagation of our species. Men are funny because they must be, so women will fuck them; conversely, men desire nearly all women, thus women don't have to try hard to impress. Hitchens magnanimously asked for contributions from famous funny women for his essay, and I find Fran Lebowitz's most incisive. Humor is both appropriative and at its core threatening, she suggests, the implication being that these traits are traditionally male. She tacitly agrees that, yes, men are considered funnier than women, because men create the culture where wit is their primary social goal. They're the curators of wit. By extension, if women want to be funny, they must behave or speak in ways that reflect that curation. Hitchens admits this himself, saying most female comedians who are indisputably funny fall into one of three (or a combo) of the following qualities: fat, queer, or Jewish. By queer, of course, he doesn't mean exclusively homosexual or sexually anomalous; he means manly. In other words, he's saying these types of crude women are unattractive to me, and only in that dearth of attraction can I accept female humor. I was heavier in my college days; this categorization was likely a prerequisite for allowing the TKEs to laugh along with me.

But there's something implicit in what Hitchens wrote that he doesn't outright acknowledge. Men would *prefer* if women weren't funny because humor has long been their realm, and they'd rather not be outdone. Humor is subversion, it's irony, it's darkness, and really, it's pain. Men would prefer if women exuded the absence of pain, which is comfort—be their shelter from the storm, rather than the storm itself. When women defy that, when they desire to make men laugh instead of, or in addition to, making them come, funny women get labeled mannish. For much of the history of humor, it's been impossible to be funny in a particularly feminine way.

Maybe it's the girl's girl mindset I've adapted with age, but I believe it's a woman's duty to be funny. Because as Jerry Seinfeld noted in a recent interview with Marc Maron, humor, at its deepest core, comes from a place of anger. Who's angrier than a twenty-first-century woman? Especially an American woman, especially my fellow women of color, who are *of course* considered equal, duh; it's why you don't *need* the Equal Rights Amendment, you dumb cunts; you're already there; you have nothing to bitch about anymore. But meanwhile please remain cool but also hot and smart, but not too smart, and if you desire power, you basically want to be a man, and please ignore that perpetual likability scale hanging over your head, and don't even try it: you will never be as funny as a man. It's all so maddening, really, it's laughable.

Sally Field remains cute in her seventies and subtly funny in a way neither Hitchens nor TKEs would recognize. In her memoir, *In Pieces*, she describes how her 1970s bandit boyfriend, Burt Reynolds, once demanded she stop cursing. During that time, she learned to say "darned" a lot. And this line—that she needed this ameliorative "darned" to retain some semblance of who she'd been—terrified me. Nearly every woman I know has subsumed a part of herself to either romantically or professionally please a man. I had promised myself at some point that I'd never stop cursing, stop being myself, for any man.

Though in reading Field's memoir, I had to ask myself, hadn't I *started* cursing for men? So I could be a guy's girl, using a language inculcated by my father, to be warmly invited into every beer-canpyramided room? So then, who was I trying to be now? Was the *cursing me* I'd constructed long ago the *actual me*? Did I truly still love to curse or just want my audience to think I loved it? I know it's still part of my anger reflex. When faced with someone who pisses me off, even during my swear abstention, I inwardly call them a "cunt."

But why "cunt"? It's the one word I won't even whisper in front of my daughter, even though it's my favorite. I like floating it before an audience I trust, because even my closest friends jolt when hearing it. "What's so wrong with 'cunt'?" I've asked. I realize it's been intimated our whole lives that it's the most awful word, but why does my social circle think so? What distinguishes it from "pussy," which roughly scores a few notches lower on the appalling scale? When polled, most friends told me they associated "cunt" with meanness, a word they'd loathe to be called or ever want their children to say. One colleague said it felt antifeminist, even after I countered with poet Heather McHugh's considerably feminist "I Knew I'd Sing," a self-proclaimed praise of that word with teeth, that word that accepts no vanilla "vagina" surrogate. My officemate said that since we'd become friends, she didn't think of it so much as a curse anymore, but more *my* word, one I could slip into a sentence decrying wilted lettuce, or in the context of a global pandemic.

Once upon a millennium, "cunt" was more ubiquitous and pragmatic. Dating back to the Middle Ages, it was used widely in medical manuals and as place-names, such as the aptly titled Gropecunt Lane, part of thirteenth-century London's brothel district. But in the post-Enlightenment, pre-Victorian eras, attitudes changed. In his 1811 *Classical Dictionary of the Vulgar Tongue*, author Francis Grose deemed the word, and the anatomy it connotes, as nasty. And in his seminal 1755 *Dictionary of the English Language*, Samuel Johnson left out the word altogether. This lack of representation snowballs over time, giving the word even more power through abstention. "Pussy" has never been silenced, because in feline contexts, it's still as conceivably pure as a pussy licking milk from a bowl. Or something like that.

In the 1990s, third-wave feminism attempted to reclaim "cunt" with two literary and cultural milestones. The first was *The Vagina Monologues*, where it became a sexy siren song. The actress delivering the "cunt" monologue seductively licks a Blow-Pop or her fingers or the microphone, but saying or thinking "cunt" does not make me want to fuck. For me, the impulse to say it comes from a need to elevate a fight, to say what the other person won't, and having the balls to say it first releases that bellicosity. Given the opportunity to "cunt" it out, I feel calmer, ready to face adversaries, real or perceived, more rationally.

The second reclamation was Inga Muscio's 1998 book, *Cunt: A Declaration of Independence*, where she argues convincingly that part of the word's verboten nature comes from women's self-hatred of our "anatomical jewel." The book further calls for women's reappropriation of the word as linchpin of female genius and beauty, much as Black hip-hop artists have done with the n-word. And while I agree I'd love for "cunt" to represent the vastness that is womanhood, while I'd like it to become "good," I still need its darker powers as well. I want it to astonish and scare, to comfort and cajole. I want not to give a fuck who likes if we use it or not.

I witnessed an example of "cunt" power a few months ago, when watching season four of Pamela Adlon's *Better Things*. I snapped into recognition during a scene where Adlon's character, Sam, argues with her oldest teenage daughter, Max. It was that typical mother/daughter "why don't you grow up/why can't you understand me" fight I've experienced countless times with my own mother and am already anticipating with my daughter. In the scene, the two women call each other "cunt," back and forth, fourteen times. The scene ends with apologies, each of them admitting, as ardently as they'd accused each other, to their *own* cuntiness. If we're being honest about any of our complicated female relationships, no truer exchange has ever been televised.

In his 1972 comedy monologue, George Carlin famously noted the seven words you can't say on television—the words we've decided, for arbitrary reasons, are our language's worst. Those words are, in no particular order, shit, piss, fuck, cocksucker, motherfucker, tits, and cunt. In the nearly fifty years since the airing of this comedy special, three of those words have already fallen from this forbidden upper echelon. Who really cares about the words "piss" or "tits," or, unless you're my daughter's tight-ass teacher, a little "shit"? Yet even though television itself and the people watching it have radically transformed since then, the other swear words on Carlin's list, especially "cunt," remain worst of the worst.

Since then we've culturally acknowledged there are more abhorrent words, like the aforementioned racial epithets. But how can anyone feel *good* saying those words? I wonder if racists lower their blood pressure by using racial epithets, if it's some kind of a deliverance for them or if it inculcates more hate, higher blood pressure, heart disease, and early deaths (in which case, shouldn't they keep using them?). Because I feel great physical and emotional relief after saying "cunt." There's less animosity toward my target and more love for myself. Is it possible "cunt" makes the world, at least for me, a better place?

My thirty-day abstention from cursing went okay. I did lots of slow breathing and stopped in the middle of sentences when a swear burbled. I was most tested during class when my Mac Daddy student read aloud from his essay-in-progress about his foray with abstinence that, according to him, had devolved into a failed venture. He recounted long conversations with his penis and how it finally won the argument when my student logged onto Tinder and swiped sideways to search for "the quickest pussy I could find." I paused to reflect on his use of "pussy" rather than "cunt," since the former is indeed more appropriate in a sexual context.

I had no idea how to respond to this work, though I ended up not having to. My Jersey girl said, "What the fuck, bro!" To which I said, "You took the words right out of my mouth."

I'm not sure what any of us learned through immersion. I already knew to be careful with my audience when cursing. And not to do it so much in front of my child, especially the worst words, especially "cunt." I became slightly more comfortable in silences between speech, to be more patient when seeking the appropriate word rather than the first one that pops to my head. That's always a good lesson, both for writing and for being a human.

It's funny to think I wouldn't stop cursing for a man, but I did try, for my daughter. And what do I want her to know about cursing? I want her to understand the curse as akin to decadent dessert—you can't have it whenever. Even though it's delicious, even though when you graduate and leave home there'll be the seduction of eating dessert for every meal. But there's a whole lexicon waiting to be opened, and I want her to be as excited to learn the meaning of "sansculotte," the current word-of-the-day in my inbox, and thousands of yet-to-be-discovered words, as she is about the versatility of "cunt." It's saying something that after centuries of being excluded from dictionaries entirely, the adjectives "cunted," "cunting," "cuntish," and "cunty" were added to the *Oxford English Dictionary* in March 2014. As I've known for a long time, the word is damn useful.

I conducted my noncursing enterprise, and started writing this essay, to decide whether I'll quit cursing for good. I'm still trying to curb swears in general, but I'm likely sticking with "cunt." Because if this isn't The Age of Cunt, I don't know what is. Cut the word "country" in half and what do you get? A big, strong "cunt" to start, then the whimper of a chopped "tree." It's the first syllable that best epitomizes where we've been, where we're going, who we are. As Americans we've been metaphorically chopped in two for our entire existence, so let's linger on the first syllable of our collective patriotism. Cunt is meanness. It's the toppling of that tree. The tree, and all the innocence and knowledge and renewal it connotes, is an American farce. Our country is, indeed, cunty. That we can say and do so many terrible things to the weakest among us, and let them go unacknowledged or denied, but clutch our pearls about "cunt," is another example so maddening it's laughable.

My incentive to curb "cunt" would be if we stopped being cunty. Last year at my annual checkup, my doctor noted how well I was doing physically after a difficult pregnancy. "You've really bounced back. What's your secret?" I toyed with my phone, where prior to her entering the exam room, I'd been reading about the ever-terrifying machinations of the ex-president's administration. The whole rot of them, cunts, I'd thought. I hope their dicks catch Covid-19 because they're cunts. Cunts, cunts, cunts, cunts on TV, was my inner monologue before the nurse took my blood pressure. It was that simple—it felt good to say, and to think about saying. "I've been exercising, practicing yoga," I lied. The truth is when I feel the need, I say "cunt," liberally. I remain in great health.

NOLA FACE

It was unfortunate: the bitch had an ugly face. Aquiline nose, weird on a dog, and muddy eyes that couldn't pick a color. Puppies are supposed to be cuddly, but her tiny cask torso was covered with coarse fur about as soft as a pinecone. When Brock rescued this abandoned pit-boxer mutt from the LSU lakes biking path shortly after Hurricane Katrina, rather than lauding his heroism, I took it personally. We already had a dog, King, a downy-soft, smiley, but high-maintenance three-year-old Aussie—when did I cosign for two? Our community was dog-rescue fatigued after the storm, so no one would take her in. If she wasn't adopted within weeks at the overrun shelter, they would, you know, kill her. King kept lovingly licking her eyes. Brock fed her by hand. Everyone was smitten, but I was already tired. When her heavy tail banged across her crate each morning before dawn, excited for another day on this Earth, I reminded her that she was alive not only because of Brock, but because of me.

Still, I'm not that shallow. Nola, whom we named perhaps too obviously after my birthplace, eventually became beautiful to me. She grew quickly into a fifty-pound pinecone, but even to old age, she behaved like a lapdog. This was a dog who conspicuously licked her lips each time we ate, tonguing bigger and bigger circles around her mouth until we offered her any little scrap of beef jerky or potato salad or oatmeal: she was easily appeased. In those early days as a sleep-deprived mom to a toddler puppy, I yelled at her a lot, but she never held a grudge. Maybe because she was so sweet, I no longer noticed her dearth of beauty. Then we moved to Alabama and, at a start-of-semester cookout we hosted, Nola met our colleagues' blonde pit bull, Purl. This dog was a Nola leveled up, a pretty Nola, smooth-and-shiny skinned with marbled muscles. A purebred.

As soon as Purl stepped confidently into the side door of our cabin, Nola lost all of her shit. She barked maniacally, hackles spiking dangerously from her back. It was like watching Gizmo morph into a Gremlin. When I pinned her down, middle-school-wrestler style, I saw the utter transformation of her face. She was a wooden-statue warrior come to life. Her nostrils flared, her eyes lasered onto Purl. She responded to no command until our colleagues finally walked backward out of the house, leaving Purl leashed and socially distanced for the next two hours.

The cookout was still a success, but we had to keep Nola crated for most of it. Her face would return to normal, but whenever Purl made an unexpected movement or sound, she'd Nola Face it all over again. That's what we called this phenomenon, the Nola Face. We had no idea how prolifically it would return when she'd encounter Daisy, the urbane French bulldog, then Sadie, the velvet-bowed, wool-sweatered terrier, then the anonymous Siberian Husky ice queen at the local arboretum. And it continued with every beautiful, purebred—or plain pretty—female dog she came across until the day, several years later, she died.

When and how had I created Nola in my own jealous, bitchy image?

Listen, I haven't been looking forward to admitting my blonde problem. It's as shamefully a part of me as my propensity to turn silently sour when I don't get my way. My dark skin and hair and reading obsession designated me early on (at least in my own mind) as culturally Not Beautiful, which gave me access to that other realm for awkward girls, Chubby/Funny. But I couldn't even be notable at that. I wasn't chubby enough for my pediatrician to scold my mother about it, and I've never been as funny as I'd like. Only last year, when my daughter started doing it and I noticed how ineffective it is, did I stop telling a joke twice if no one laughed after my first delivery (*I'll change my inflection this time, then they'll get it!*). Funny people are supposed to let shit go more easily, but I'm no Tina Fey. In her book *Bossypants*, Fey readily dispatches the power of blondes by calling them "yellow hairs." By renaming them something so prosaic, she chops off their mystical powers. And in an age when standard beauty norms have changed drastically, when in my teens, Selena and J-Lo widened them, I couldn't blame a reader for wondering what the hell my problem is.

But it cannot be helped. Blondes are, for me, Elijah Mohammed's white devil. They're the white devil's daughter. They are the standard, they are the ultimate, they are the totally tubular. They are Christie Brinkley lithely dancing before a red Corvette while Chevy Chase throws her sandwich air-kisses, they are Olivia Newton-John in black leather and Aqua-Netted curls, they are a size negative o Penny shimmying in *Dirty Dancing*, in all her preabortion, pink-dressed perfection. They are Christie Brinkley, again, fancy-hatted and descending from a Black-butler-driven Rolls Royce, twirling with a bunch of mechanics singing Doo Wop into socket wrenches, and because one of them is Billy Joel, despite all of them making rape-y faces at her, she knows for certain she is not going to get raped.

To exorcise myself from their dominion over my childhood, I recently decided to reimmerse in early eighties blondes, and it was the 1983 music video for "Uptown Girl" that ultimately broke the spell. I cannot believe I ever coveted these blondes' looks or lives. They are skinny and boring and, barring Penny's abortion snafu, soullessly one-dimensional. Their personality is "I like boys," though they like even better for boys to notice them. Yet this is inherent to the blonde problem: their dearth of character doesn't matter. Because they were, and remain, ubiquitous. Only after reading Claudia Rankine's essay "Complicit Freedoms" in her collection *Just Us*, did I discover blondes' ubiquity is a facade. It turns out hardly 2 percent of the world's blondes are naturally so; real blondes live in Sweden, and the rest of them dye it. The possibility that many blondes are originally brunettes who might also hate themselves has provided me no small amount of comfort.

I'd always assumed my blonde issue was a beauty thing. Because if there's an American caste system for beauty, and of course there is, I grew up solidly middle caste, destined to always venerate yellow hairs as beacons of sublimity. To some degree that's still true. But in years of studying Nola's Nola Face directed pointedly to *purebred* female dogs, I'm seeing a connection in our Nolafacedness. Nola and I are both muddled mutts. We lack purity. Or perhaps a better word for it: pedigree.

It was not the case that every one of my graduate school peers were moneyed white people with advanced degree'd parents. But most of them were. It's true, a small number felt proud to call themselves blue collar, like the New England white woman who also claimed to be more Hispanic than me (Her rationale: I couldn't cumbia, and she grew up with more Hispanic friends. For the record, she was a blue-eyed blonde. Ain't that a bitch?). No one in grad school ever explicitly stated this, of course, but implicit in feedback I received (there were correct ways to interpret, apparently, my Ecuadorian grandmother's culture and behaviors), in the canonical readings I was assigned, was that whites had more of a right to write. My imaginary readers looked like the crowd of lilies surrounding me at the mahogany table in the Robert Penn Warren Room, so I bent a quiet head across the workshop table toward them.

What graduate school conferred—much more than learning the craft of writing—was a tentative access to pedigree that I wouldn't have had otherwise. Because being first-gen is mere novelty; real pedigree trumps it every time. Sure, with an MFA in hand, I could teach as an instructor at a university but would be paid half the salary of my tenure-track colleagues and teach twice as much. The real access gained was in accumulating academic friends for whom the intellectual life I've always coveted was a given.

One good friend worked in upper administration at the University of Alabama; her father was college president for another large, southern state school. This meant their family lived in the campus mansion, where once, in my early thirties, I was invited to stay for a weekend. Their house/museum was decorated with inscrutable paintings by canonical artists I couldn't name and would forget to later look up. If family pedigree could be ascertained by furniture, this one was Brazilian mahogany. Mine was Walmart particle board.

A decade later, this lovely and welcoming family remain dear friends, but imagine you grew up with a stepfather who considered the height of literature to be *Field and Stream*, best read on the toilet with a Busch Light, and you've entered the colonial home belonging to the better-adjusted Tenenbaums. Every family member had a Major Artistic Talent—singing, painting, dancing—and probably even their dog knew which artists hung on the walls. What stung the most is that everyone spoke Spanish, since they'd traveled the world many times over, vacationed in Spain and Mexico and across South America. Study abroad was not an "if" concept, but a when, where, and how often. I scanned photos atop the mahogany sideboard (a piece of furniture which I only later learned the name of) and saw a picture of my friend's father and stepmother. With the pope.

The stately stepmother lifted the gilded frame. "We were lucky enough to be visiting the Vatican when he came out to bless the crowd. And he sure was holy, because I got pregnant right after this trip! That's why we named our oldest Maria Graciela."

Before I could sink my ass into some genuine leather, the father poured me a bourbon neat. This was a language I fully understood. But then he started speaking to me in Spanish, declaring how lucky I was to grow up around it.

"Yup," I said.

"En español!" he said, merrily.

Because I've historically done precisely what white men ask me to, I stumbled through some excuse for my poor Spanish. My grandmother was in a nursing home in New Orleans, and she wasn't much for talking on the phone anymore.

"What about your mother?" he asked.

"Oh, we've never spoken Spanish with each other. That would be like us flossing each other's teeth. Unnatural." I hoped my jokes were making up for the fact I was continuing to speak in English, while he spoke in Spanish. How long could this continue? Unnatural, indeed.

"Have you been back to the homeland yet? Es Ecuador, si?" he asked.

"Not yet, unfortunately."

"Oh, you must go! Why haven't you?"

"*Muy pobre*" would've been an honest, easy response. Expedia tickets cost more than a grand no matter the season. But I would also need to bone up on my Spanish beforehand to avoid situations like the one I was in right now. I didn't want to sound like an Enriquita in front of any long-lost relatives. I gave another noncommittal (but truthful) answer.

"No se."

I thought that would be the low point in this trip's Nola Facery, begrudging nice, overly educated white people for their nice, overly educated white lives. But then I learned about the eleven-year-old twins' Major Artistic Talent: writing. I don't have Nola's hackles, but I did feel the hair rise on the back of my neck when I heard this unwelcome news.

The twins had won separate statewide writing competitions, the stepmother announced. She knew I was a writer and insisted I appraise their work. After I read one of their poems, something melancholic, highly skilled and, yes, well beyond their ages, I smiled and offered encouragement. Meanwhile, my emotional hackles lowered because I could finally relax. My shit was better than theirs. That's when I knew I must beg Nola's forgiveness for my years of judgment. I had a major Nola Face problem of my own.

Part of the problem with New Orleans itself is that while its residents pride themselves on the culture, the food, their inherent warmth, they're obsessed with pedigree too. Where you're from within the city matters. So many times I've been asked by both natives and transplants a simple enough question: *Where in Nola did you grow up?* But deeper into my thirties, I realized what an in-crowd question this is. At a poetry festival in the Marigny, the impossibly hip, gentrified neighborhood bordering the French Quarter's north end, a poet (blonde) asked me this question. I gave my noncommittal "from all over" response, but then she pressed, "yeah, but where did you go to high school?" I answered truthfully—the largest public high school in the state of Louisiana, located on the Westbank, home to a decent football team and not-too-big-of-a-race-riot the day of the O. J. Simpson verdict—and she said, "Oh." And sipped her Tom Collins, and turned away. My "from all over" answer is the quickest. But if we're gonna get into it, I'm from a lot of specific places in New Orleans. Though none of them are the "good," recognizable ones that paint the mystique of the city.

I'm from New Orleans East, Michoud Boulevard, where Lala lived. Her house was one of the few without barred windows, a detriment on the morning Lala's lawn boy endeavored to break in with a crowbar. Luckily, two loud sounds scared him away: Lala's hysterical Spanish curses, and her dog Titina's barking. I suppose we're all fearful of what we can't see, which is why I'm grateful the guy didn't know that on our side of the brick wall, Lala held only a broom and a foreign language to defend us. Titina, for her part, was a Bichon Frise who'd been blind since before my birth.

I'm from Lakeview, site of the once-grand Pontchartrain Park, which closed due to high levels of water toxicity right around the time I would've enjoyed it. Lakeview is where I met my first stepfather, who introduced me to the word "primadonna." It makes sense now, that he'd given me this name, since I'd ask him delightful questions like, "Did you even go to college?" When I heard my mother and him arguing about me, I believed the word was a different kind of insult, pre-Madonna, something akin to "precool." I was in my twenties when I learned the word's definition, and it was ironic that I'd been calling him a dumbass without understanding what he was calling me. Lakeview was also where I first learned about death. Two goldfish, back-to-back, committed suicide by jumping out of their bowl into my room's trashcan. I became inured to funerals ending in flushes, and wondered if their final resting place would be the lake I'd never get to swim in.

I'm from Metairie, French for "white flight," the district that elected the convicted felon and former KKK Grand Wizard (and current Trump succubus) David Duke to the Louisiana House of Representatives in 1989. Toward the end of Duke's ignominious term, in 1992, Hurricane Andrew hit Louisiana's boot sole, and the drainage canal at the end of our street overflowed, sending gators and snakes past our house. We neighborhood kids swam in the streets until those nonpolitician reptiles got too close.

I'm from the Westbank, across the river from New Orleans proper, where I learned to speak a third language—Westbankese—full of *bruh* and *where yat* and *youse a pussy ass bitch*. It took me awhile to get the hang of this new manner of speaking. My first day of junior high gym class, a boy asked me if I had talked to another boy. Just like that, he said, "You talking to him?" I said, yes, I'd talked to him earlier. By the end of the day I understood "talking to" meant "dating," and clarifying to the boy and my peers that I wasn't interested (and didn't know what I was saying earlier) was kind of like admitting I was a Latina who didn't speak Spanish well. My family moved to the Westbank as I started ninth grade, and this event coincided with the dispassionate loss of my virginity. I don't blame this loss on my backyard swampland that forced me and the neighbor boy inside during most months of the year. The lovebugs were so fervent in their own dispassionate fucking that I had to kick the front door to shoo them away enough for me to get inside my home every day after school.

Point is, I don't have an easy answer to where I'm from in New Orleans, and I certainly don't have the right answer. Because the right answers could be the dazzling French Quarter or cool Marigny or Bywater or even the bustling Central Business District. But the *best* right answer is Uptown. When you're Uptown, you're an insider. Kind of like one of my grad school friends, originally from Idaho, who cooked a shit-ton of amuse-bouche at a French brasserie while he attended the private university Loyola. Yeah, he was Uptown. He knew where all the hip restaurants were, who to call for coke or MDMA. I'd never even walked a second line! "You're not real New Orleans," he's ribbed me more than once. And because I didn't have access to what he knew about my city, he was right. (Though I discovered years later how close I was to being an Uptown girl myself. When they were

married in the late seventies, my mother and father lived in an Uptown duplex on Fountainbleu, where they owned two pet birds whose
names were, no shit, Billy and Joel.)

Nola knew my latest iteration, New-Mother-Rage-Fear-Fuck Face,
for over a year before she died. Lots is written and, I'd contend, lied
about with respect to dog owners integrating children into their home.
As in, new parents actually make some kind of effort. We tried none
of that, but then again, maybe we were inordinately lucky for our two
dogs' willingness to embrace the baby. Nola especially needed no in-
troductions. My daughter's first picture at home prominently features
Nola's tongue licking the entire left side of her newborn face. Still, *my*
new face couldn't accept the love. I conjured fervid ruminations of
slapstick Nola insanity leading to my daughter's sudden death. Like,
Nola might be nestling behind me while I held my daughter, then I'd
step back, trip over the stupid dog, and the baby would go flying and
smack into the wall with a sick thud, her little life snuffed out because
of a stupid dog's incautious nestling habits. Or I'd be attempting to finally eat when Nola, stupid dog, would jump several feet in the air,
Looney-Tunes style, at the sound of a FedEx truck and the fork I was
holding would jam into my baby's eye. I imagined, you know, incredibly normal shit like that. I thought "stupid dog" many times in Nola's final year of life, and "stupid bitch" too, when considering myself. For her part, Nola never held me to account for my own lunacy
or bitchiness. Ever the masochist, she licked and loved me vocifer-
ously till the end.

The last time I saw Nola's face was the day after Christmas in 2016.
We'd hired a dog sitter in Tuscaloosa so we could have a more peaceful Christmas with our baby at my mother's house in New Orleans.
The dogsitter unintentionally left our front door open—I still don't
know the whole story—and Nola wandered away. We found her two
days later, apparently having been struck and killed by a car on Lur-
leen Wallace Highway, several blocks from our home and a few yards
away from the Sonic Drive-In, her sweet pink tongue hanging from

her mouth. Brock buried her in our backyard, heroically, in the cold December rain.

I often wonder about that last night of Nola's life. She must've been terrified. It was cold and she was alone and didn't know how to find home. That's the closest version to the truth I can conjure, and I fucking hate it.

But I've got a version of that night I like better. Her parents were gone, so Nola was going to take advantage. She was hungry. Four blocks over, the cheese-meat smell of Sonic called. Why should those cunty purebreds, the ones who don't even have to lick their lips to get want they want, have all the fun? Nola was gonna get her ass some Sonic. She pointed her beautiful, aquiline nose toward her desire: a perfect, hardly eaten, quarter-pound double cheeseburger some chump had thrown out their car window. Nola got hold of it, a full, meaty bite. She was, at that moment, like the city of my birth: even on the precipice of disaster, chomping away, enjoying the things in life that are good.

Seeing Nola's face in mine, or mine in hers, gave me the confidence to be myself, to own my feelings as a writer and daughter and mother and wife, even if the feelings were juvenile or shameful. Because they were true. Her love wasn't the grandest I've ever experienced—Lala's love holds that title—but Nola's no-reservations love is most aspirational. No matter what face I wore, she sought me for a nuzzle or a kiss. Yes, that may be masochism, or dog-ism, or maybe it's just a creature who gives all of themselves for others. That kind of love is emblematic of the city that raised me and the people who raised me in it.

Despite this newfound confidence, I'll never be sure how qualified I am to write about the city of my birth, the nature of my insecurities, the nature of anything. If I'm legit New Orleans enough to write about New Orleans. Or Latina enough to write about being Latina. Or too pretty to write about feeling ugly, or too dumb to write about smart things, but also too keenly self-sabotaging to tell the truth, simple and plain. I don't know if I'll ever be able to fully rid myself of the Nola Face that was so obvious in my dog, and within myself. But whether or not I've learned anything, sometime while I was hardly noticing it, Nola's face—the Nola Face—became smart, became beautiful, became mine.

Nola Face